FRENCH IS FUN

FRENCH IS FUN

Lively Lessons for Beginners

GAIL STEIN
Teacher of French

HEYWOOD WALD, Ph.D.
Assistant Principal

Foreign Language Department
Martin Van Buren High School
New York City

Dedicated to serving

AMSCO

our nation's youth

When ordering this book, please specify *either* R 283 W *or* FRENCH IS FUN

AMSCO SCHOOL PUBLICATIONS, INC.
315 Hudson Street / New York, N.Y. 10013

OTHER BOOKS IN THIS SERIES:

Italian Is Fun
Spanish Is Fun

Illustrations by Louise Ann Uher

ISBN 0-87720-450-0

Copyright © 1985 by Amsco School Publications, Inc.

Printed in the United States of America

Preface

FRENCH IS FUN provides an introductory program that makes language acquisition a natural, personalized, enjoyable, and rewarding experience.

FRENCH IS FUN is designed to help students attain an acceptable level of proficiency in four basic skills—listening, speaking, reading, and writing—developed through simple materials in visually focused contexts that students can easily relate to their own experiences. Students are asked easy-to-answer questions that require them to speak about their daily lives, express their opinions, and supply real information.

Since this worktext provides all the elements for a one-year course, it can be used as the primary text.

FRENCH IS FUN consists of six parts. Each part contains four lessons, followed by a *Révision* unit, in which structure and vocabulary are recapitulated and practiced through various *activités*. These include games and puzzles as well as more conventional types of exercises. Lessons 12 and 24 are followed by an Achievement Test.

Each lesson includes a step-by-step sequence of the following student-directed elements, which are designed to make the materials immediately accessible as well as give students the feeling that they can have fun learning and practicing their French:

Vocabulary

Each lesson begins with thematically related sets of drawings that convey the meanings of new words in French, without recourse to English. This device enables students to make a direct and vivid association between the French terms and their meanings. The *activités* also use pictures to practice and review French words and expressions.

To facilitate comprehension, the authors use cognates of English words wherever suitable, especially in the first lesson, which is based entirely on French words that are identical to or closely resemble their English equivalents. Beginning a course in this way shows the students that French is not so "foreign" after all and helps them overcome any fears they may have about the difficulty of learning a foreign language.

Structures

FRENCH IS FUN uses a simple, straightforward, guided presentation of new structural elements. These elements are introduced in small learning components—one at a time—and are directly followed by appropriate *activités,* many of them visually cued and personalized. Students thus gain a feeling of accomplishment and success by making their own discoveries and formulating their own conclusions.

Reading

Each lesson contains a short, entertaining narrative or playlet that features new structural elements and vocabulary and reinforces previously learned grammar and expressions. These passages deal with topics that are related to the everyday experiences of today's student generation. Cognates and near-cognates are used extensively.

Conversation

To encourage students to use French for communication and self-expression, the authors have included short situational dialogs—sometimes practical, sometimes humorous—in most of the lessons. All conversations are illustrated to provide a sense of realism. Conversations are followed by dialog exercises that serve as springboards for additional personalized conversation.

Testing

The two Achievement Tests in FRENCH IS FUN are designed to be simple in order to give *all* students a sense of accomplishment. The tests show a variety of techniques through which comprehension of structure and vocabulary may be evaluated. Teachers may use them as they appear in the book or modify them to fit particular needs.

A separate *Teacher's Manual and Key* provides suggestions for teaching all elements in the book, additional practice and testing materials, and a complete key for all exercises and puzzles.

THE AUTHORS

Contents

French Pronunciation   1

Première Partie

Leçon   **1**   **Le français et l'anglais**   7
Words similar or the same in French and English. How to say "the" in French (definite article, singular).

     2   **La famille**   19
How to make things plural (definite article, plural).

     3   **La classe et l'école**   31
The indefinite articles (**un, une, des**).

     4   **La description**   43
Agreement of adjectives (singular and plural).

RÉVISION I (Leçons 1–4)   58

Deuxième Partie

     5   **Les verbes**   65
Words that express action. **-ER** verbs.

     6   **Encore des verbes**   77
More **-ER** verbs. How to ask a question and say "no" in French.

     7   **Un, deux, trois . . .**   90
How to count in French (numbers 1–39).

     8   **Les verbes continuent**   97
More action words. **-IR** verbs.

RÉVISION II (Leçons 5–8)   103

Troisième Partie

     9   **"To be or not to be"**   115
The verb **être.** Professions.

     10   **Encore des verbes**   125
-RE verbs.

     11   **Les parties du corps**   133
The verb **avoir.** Expressions with **avoir.**

12 Les jours, les mois, les saisons   149
RÉVISION III (Leçons 9–12)   159
ACHIEVEMENT TEST I (Leçons 1–12)   167

Quatrième Partie

13 Les aliments   175
The partitive.
14 Quelle heure est-il?   188
Telling time in French.
15 C'est ma maison   202
Possessive adjectives.
16 Le couvert   215
Demonstrative adjectives.
RÉVISION IV (Leçons 13–16)   224

Cinquième Partie

17 Les numéros   233
Numbers to 100.
18 Les lieux   239
Places to go and speak about. Contractions.
19 Allons-y!   249
The verb **aller.**
20 Quel temps fait-il?   261
Seasons and weather. The verb **faire.**
RÉVISION V (Leçons 17–20)   270

Sixième Partie

21 Vouloir et pouvoir   281
22 Les vêtements; les couleurs   292
Position of adjectives.
23 Les animaux   302
The verb **voir.**
24 Je suis américain. Je suis américaine.   314
Nationalities, countries, and languages.
RÉVISION VI (Leçons 21–24)   325
ACHIEVEMENT TEST II (Leçons 13–24)   331

Vocabulaire français-anglais   339
Vocabulaire anglais-français   348

Index   357

FRENCH
IS FUN

French Pronunciation

Some French letters are pronounced more or less the way they are in English. Some, however, are quite different. When you are in doubt, you can refer to this table.

VOWEL SOUNDS

FRENCH LETTERS	ENGLISH SOUND	EXAMPLES
a	ah (mama)	la
e	uh (until)	je
é, final -er, final -ez, et	ay (day)	musée, parler, adorez, et
e + two consonants, ê, è, e + final pronounced consonant	eh (ever)	mettre, sept, être, élève
eu	There is no English sound equivalent. Round your lips and try saying eh at the same time.	deux
eu, oeu	i (sir)	seul, soeur
i (î), y	ee (meet)	il, île, Sylvie
i + vowel, ill	y (yes)	étudier, fille, famille
o + final pronounced consonant	uh (up)	homme
ô, au, eau, o last sound of word and before -se	oh (open)	bientôt, au, eau, radio, rose
ou	oo (tooth)	où
oi, oî	wa (watch)	trois
u	There is no English sound equivalent. Round your lips and try saying ee at the same time.	tu
u + vowel	we (we)	huit, suis

h	**h** at the beginning of a word is silent; therefore, all words that begin with an **h** begin with a vowel sound.	**h**ôtel

CONSONANT SOUNDS

In French, most final consonants are not pronounced except for final **C, F, L,** and **R**.

FRENCH LETTERS	ENGLISH SOUND	EXAMPLES
c (before **e, i, y**)	s	**c**e, **c**igarette, Nan**c**y
ç (before **a, o, u**)	s	**ç**a, gar**ç**on,
c (before **a, o. u**)	k	**c**arotte, **c**omme, **c**urieux
ch	sh	**ch**ez, Mi**ch**el
j, g (before **e, i, y**)	similar to zh	**j**e, rou**g**e, **J**im, **g**igantesque
ge (before **a, o**)	similar to zh	man**ge**ons
g (before **a, o, u**)	g (hard g)	**g**ant, **g**omme
qu, final **q**	k	**qu**e, cin**q**
ss	s	poi**ss**on, de**ss**ert
s at beginning of word, **s** before a consonant	s	**s**ix di**s**que
s between vowels	z	poi**s**on, dé**s**ert
th	t	**th**é, **th**éâtre
x	x	e**x**cellent, e**x**pert
x	s	only in si**x**, di**x**, soi**x**ante

NASAL SOUNDS

Nasal sounds are produced by emitting breath through the nose and mouth at the same time. Nasal sounds occur when you have VOWEL + N or M. Be careful, there is no nasal sound for VOWEL + NM

             VOWEL + MM

             VOWEL + N/M + VOWEL

NASAL COMBINATIONS	EXAMPLES
an en **am em**	France, Henri lampe, embrasse
in ain **im aim**	industrie, pain important, faim
ien	bien
on om	bon, bombe
un um	lundi, parfum

LIAISON AND ELISION

Liaison and elision are two pronunciation techniques that make the French language sound so beautiful. What are they? Let's start with liaison. In French, the final consonant of a word is usually NOT pronounced. Sometimes, however, we do pronounce this final consonant. See if you can determine when:

les amis
z

nous arrivons
z

sept hommes
t

Liaison means linking one word with the word that follows it. For a liaison to occur, we link the final consonant sound of the first word with the beginning vowel sound of the word that follows it.

Next, let's discuss elision. Elision means dropping a vowel sound (usually **e** or **i**) at the end of one word if the next word begins with a vowel sound. The vowel that we drop can't just disappear, it must be replaced by an apostrophe. You will most often have elision with the final **e** of **je, ne, de que**:

Je arrive = **J'arrive**
Il ne étudie pas = Il **n'étudie** pas
La classe de histoire = La classe **d'histoire**
Que est-ce que = **Qu'est**-ce que

Première Partie

1 | Le français et l'anglais

1 So, you're starting to learn French. **Magnifique.** You'll have a lot of fun learning French, and it won't really be that hard. Do you know why? Well, there are lots of words that are identical in both the English and French languages. Sure, they may be pronounced differently, but they are spelled the same way and have exactly the same meaning. Also, there are many words that have a slightly different spelling (often just one letter) but can be recognized instantly by anyone who speaks English.

O.K. Let's look at some of them and pronounce them the French way after your teacher has done so.

Words that are exactly the same in English and French:

blond	la blouse	le boulevard	l'accident
certain	la boutique	le bureau	l'âge
cruel	la nation	le café	l'animal
différent	la photo	le chef	l'automobile
élégant	la phrase	le client	l'avenue
excellent	la question	le cousin	l'éléphant
horrible	la radio	le fruit	l'hôtel
immense	la région	le guide	l'océan
important	la table	le menu	
intelligent	la télévision	le parent	
orange		le président	
sincère		le pullover	
		le restaurant	
		le sandwich	
		le snack-bar	
		le sport	
		le téléphone	
		le ticket	
		le train	
		le village	
		le voyage	
		le zoo	

Here are some French words which look *almost* like English words. Repeat them in French after your teacher:

africain	la bicyclette	le bébé	l'acteur
américain	la biologie	le criminel	l'algèbre
bleu	la carotte	le directeur	l'anniversaire
canadien	la cathédrale	le docteur	l'appartement
charmant	la céréale	le jardin	l'artiste
confortable	la classe	le lac	l'employé
délicieux	la danse	le monstre	l'enfant
enchanté	la famille	le moteur	l'ennemi
grillé	la guitare	le paragraphe	l'exercice
intéressant	la lampe	le parc	l'histoire
italien	la leçon	le professeur	l'hôpital
mexicain	la liste	le programme	l'île
moderne	la maman	le théâtre	l'oncle
nécessaire	la musique	le tigre	l'université
ordinaire	la personne	le touriste	
populaire	la salade	le verbe	
riche	la soupe	le vocabulaire	
stupide	la tomate		
superbe			
tendre			
admirer			
adorer			
chanter			
danser			
imiter			
préparer			
présenter			

And, of course, there are many words that are quite different from our English vocabulary and which you must memorize. Even here, however, you'll probably be able to learn them very easily by connecting them with some similar English word.

For example: **la poule** *chicken* (*poultry*)
le disque *record* (*disk*)
l'arbre *tree* (*arbor*)
rouge *red* (*rouge*)

l'ami

l'arbre

8

 **le cinéma**

 **le dessin**

 **le disque**

 **l'école**

 **la fille**

 **le garçon**

 **le journal**

 **la maison**

 **la mère**

 **le patron**

 **le père**

la poule

 **le repas**

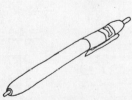 **le stylo**

 **les vacances**

le vendeur

le vin

2 Well, so much for vocabulary. Let's learn a little French grammar now. Did you notice the words **le, la, l'** before all of the nouns? These three words are the French words for "the." That's right. French has three words for "the" to describe a singular noun: **le, la,** and **l'.** The reason is that all French nouns, unlike English nouns, have a SEX or GENDER. Nouns are either MASCULINE (m.) or FEMININE (f.). Nouns also have a NUMBER. Nouns are either SINGULAR or PLURAL: **le** is used before masculine singular nouns that start with a consonant; **la** is used before feminine singular nouns that start with a consonant; **l'** is used before masculine and feminine singular nouns that start with a vowel or with **h**.

The problem is how to tell which words are masculine and which are feminine. With some words, it's very easy. Obviously, **maman, mère** (*mother*), **fille** (*girl, sister*), **femme** (*woman*) are feminine, while **père** (*father*), **garçon** (*boy*), and **homme** (*man*) are masculine. But, why is **disque** masculine and **maison** feminine? There really is no logical reason. So the only way to learn French vocabulary is with the word for "the." You don't memorize **tigre** but **le tigre**, not **musique** but **la musique**.

3 Now that we've learned some French vocabulary and grammar, let's see if we can figure out the meaning of these ten sentences. Repeat them aloud after your teacher:

1. L'hôtel est grand.

2. La classe est intelligente.

10

3. Le professeur est excellent.

4. La poule est stupide.

5. Le docteur est américain.

6. L'artiste est populaire.

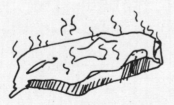

7. Le sandwich est grillé.

8. La leçon est importante.

9. La famille est riche.

10. L'appartement est confortable.

11

Formidable! Here are ten more:

1. Le président est blond.

2. L'auto est bleue.

3. L'accident est tragique.

4. Le moteur est nécessaire.

5. L'acteur est élégant.

6. Le criminel est stupide.

7. L'ami est sincère.

8. La question est intéressante.

9. L'hôpital est moderne.

10. Le menu est intéressant.

Activités

A. Match the following words with the correct pictures:

la guitare   le jardin   le stylo
la carotte   la cathédrale   le journal
la blouse   l'éléphant   la bicyclette
le bébé

1. _____

3. _____   4. _____

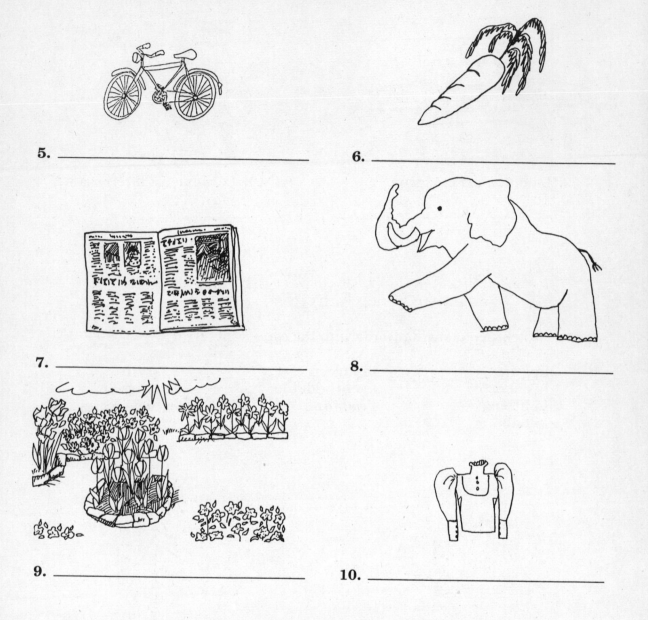

5. _____

6. _____

7. _____

8. _____

9. _____

10. _____

B. Label the following pictures. Make sure to use **le, la,** or **l'**:

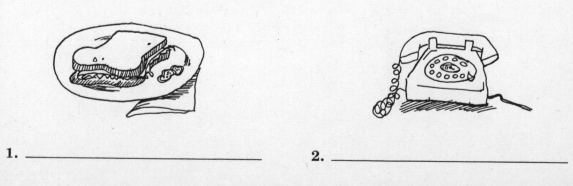

1. _____

2. _____

3. _____

4. _____

5. _____

6. _____

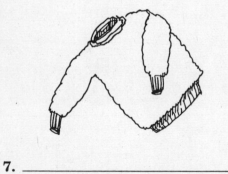

7. _____

8. _____

9. _____

10. _____

15

11. _____

12. _____

14. _____

13. _____

15. _____

16. _____

17. _____

18. _____

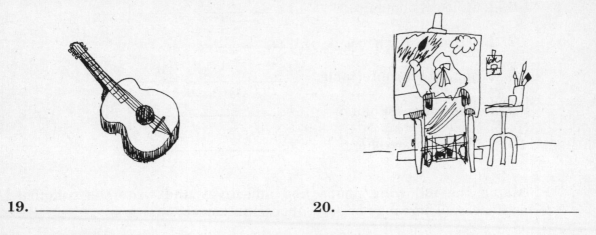

19. _____   20. _____

C. The following nouns are missing the word for "the." Place **le, la,** or **l'** before each word:

1. _____ parc   2. _____ fille

3. _____ animal   4. _____ classe

5. _____ sport   6. _____ homme

7. _____ personne   8. _____ automobile

9. _____ restaurant   10. _____ boutique

11. _____ océan   12. _____ fruit

13. _____ table   14. _____ professeur

15. _____ enfant   16. _____ bureau

17. _____ leçon   18. _____ cinéma

19. _____ famille   20. _____ jardin

D. OUI (yes) **ou NON** (no). Tell whether each statement is true (**VRAI**) or false (**FAUX**):

1. L'éléphant est rouge.   _____

2. Le criminel est charmant.   _____

3. Le tigre est stupide.   _____

4. Le professeur est riche.   _____

5. Le bébé est grand.   _____

17

6. L'école est populaire. _____

7. L'océan est immense. _____

8. L'hôpital est confortable. _____

9. Le président est blond. _____

10. La leçon est excellente. _____

E. Match the following nouns and adjectives and write the completed sentences. (There may be several possible correct answers):

1. Le professeur est _____. grillé

2. Le tigre est _____. blond

3. Le café est _____. confortable

4. Le train est _____. cruel

5. Le président est _____. grand

6. L'acteur est _____. riche

7. L'hôtel est _____. populaire

8. Le parc est _____. charmant

9. L'homme est _____. moderne

10. Le sandwich est _____. intéressant

F. Choose the words from the list that will tell others about you:

formidable	**populaire**	**stupide**
moderne	**riche**	**superbe**
ordinaire	**sincère**	**tendre**

1. Je suis _____

2. _____

3. _____

4. _____

5. _____

2 | La famille

1 Vocabulaire

la mère

la grand-mère

la soeur

la fille

le père

le grand-père

le frère

le fils

le chat

le chien

2 Here we have one big happy family. It's obvious who all the members are. Let's take a closer look:

La famille Dupont est grande. Antoine et Marie sont les grands-parents. Le père est Maurice. Qui est la mère? Janine est la mère. Charles, Michel, Denise et Claudette sont les enfants. Charles et Michel sont frères. Ils sont les fils de Maurice et de Janine. Denise et Claudette sont sœurs. Elles sont les filles de Maurice et de Janine. Il y a huit personnes dans la famille. Il y a aussi les chiens: Féroce et Terreur. Il y a aussi les chats: Tigre et Griffe. La famille est de Paris, France. Quelle famille magnifique!

est *is*
sont *are*
qui *who*
et *and*

les frères *the brothers*
  les fils *the sons*
   les sœurs *the sisters*
   les filles *the daughters*
il y a *there is, are* **huit** *eight*
aussi *also* **les chiens** *the dogs*
de *from* **quelle** *what a*

Activités

A. Match the words with the pictures:

la mère   le bébé   les soeurs
le père   le chat   les frères
le grand-père   le chien
la grand-mère   les parents

1. _____

2. _____

3. _____

4. _____

5. _____

6. _____

7. _____

8. _____

21

9. _____   10. _____

B. Fill in the blanks correctly to make the following sentences complete:

1. Janine est _____.

2. Les enfants sont _____, _____,

_____ et _____.

3. Charles est _____ de Michel.

4. Charles et Michel sont _____.

5. Antoine est _____ de Maurice.

6. Terreur et Féroce sont _____.

7. Maurice et Janine sont _____.

8. Les chats sont _____ et _____.

9. Denise est _____ de Claudette.

10. Les fils de Maurice et Janine sont _____ et

_____.

11. Les filles de Maurice et Janine sont _____ et

_____.

C. OUI ou NON: Tell whether each statement is true (**VRAI**) or false (**FAUX**). If your answer is **FAUX**, give the correct answer.

1. Le chien est **un animal**. _____

2. Le grand-père est **le frère** de Maurice. _____

3. Denise et Claudette sont **frères**. _____

22

4. Les chats sont **Terreur** et **Féroce.** _____

5. Charles et Michel sont **sœurs.** _____

6. Michel est **la fille** de Janine. _____

7. Féroce est **l'ennemi** de Tigre. _____

8. Charles est **le fils** de Maurice. _____

9. Charles et Denise sont **les parents.** _____

10. Tigre est **l'ami** de Terreur. _____

D. Fill in the correct word for "the." Choose from **le, la,** or **l':**

1. _____ père   **2.** _____ mère

3. _____ fils   **4.** _____ fille

5. _____ sœur   **6.** _____ frère

7. _____ grand-père   **8.** _____ grand-mère

9. _____ enfant   **10.** _____ famille

11. _____ chat   **12.** _____ chien

3 In this big, happy family there are many people. When we speak about more than one person or thing, we must use the PLURAL: Let's see if you can figure out the easy rules for changing most nouns (people, places, or things) to the plural. Look carefully:

I	II
le frère	les frères
le chat	les chats
le chien	les chiens
la mère	les mères
la fille	les filles
la grand-mère	les grands-mères
l'ami	les amis
l'ennemi	les ennemis
l'oncle	les oncles

Let's start by comparing the two groups of words. Underline the nouns in Groups I and II. Now look at them carefully and fill in the rest of this rule:

> In French, to make most nouns plural, simply add _____ to the
>
> _____ of the noun.

4 Now let's look at one exception to this rule:

le fils   **les fils**

How do you make a French noun plural if it already ends in **s**?

Now underline all the words in Group I that mean "the." Look carefully at Group II, do the same, and fill in the rest of the rule:

> The plural form of **le** is _____.
>
> The plural form of **la** is _____.
>
> The plural form of **l'** is _____.
>
> **les** means _____.

5 Remember, in English we have only one word for "the." How many ways are

there to say "the" in French? There are _____.

When do you use **le**? _____

la? _____

l'? _____

les? _____

Activités

E. Fill in the correct word for "the" in French. Use **le, la, l',** or **les**:

1. _____ chats   2. _____ fille

3. _____ frère   4. _____ oncle

5. _____ famille   6. _____ chien

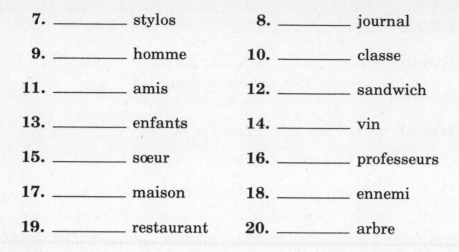

7. _____ stylos   8. _____ journal

9. _____ homme   10. _____ classe

11. _____ amis   12. _____ sandwich

13. _____ enfants   14. _____ vin

15. _____ sœur   16. _____ professeurs

17. _____ maison   18. _____ ennemi

19. _____ restaurant   20. _____ arbre

F. Make the following words plural. Use the correct form of "the":

1. la mère _____

2. le parent _____

3. l'artiste _____

4. le cinéma _____

5. la question _____

6. le théâtre _____

7. le parc _____

8. l'hôtel _____

9. l'exercice _____

10. le fils _____

11. le voyage _____

12. la liste _____

13. l'arbre _____

14. le village _____

15. le repas _____

16. le grand-père _____

17. la table _____

18. l'université _____

19. la nation _____

20. la photo _____

G. Identifiez:

1. _____

2. _____

3. _____   4. _____

5. _____   6. _____

7. _____   8. _____

9. _____   10. _____

CONVERSATION

VOCABULAIRE

bonjour *hello*
mademoiselle *miss*
monsieur *Mr., sir*
Comment vous appelez vous?
   What's your name?
Je m'appelle *My name is*
Comment allez-vous? *How are you?*

bien *fine*
merci *thanks*
et vous *and you*
à bientôt *see you soon*
à demain *till tomorrow*
au revoir *good-bye*

DIALOGUE

Fill in the correct responses in the dialog. Choose your responses from the list provided below:

_____

Bonjour, monsieur. Comment vous appelez-vous?

_____

Je m'appelle Anne. Comment allez-vous?

_____

Très bien. Au revoir, Roger.

_____

Très bien, merci. Et vous?   Je m'appelle Roger.
Bonjour, mademoiselle.   À demain, Anne.

VOUS

The Census Bureau is taking a survey. Fill out the information called for about your family:

Je m'appelle _____

Père: _____

Mère: _____

Frère(s): _____

Soeur(s): _____

Grand-père: _____

Grand-mère: _____

Chien(s): _____

Chat(s): _____

QUESTIONS PERSONNELLES

1. Comment vous appelez-vous?

_____

2. Comment allez-vous?

_____

La classe et l'école

1 Vocabulaire

Read the new words aloud after your teacher:

le professeur

le professeur

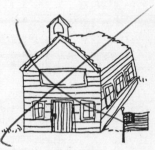

l'école

l'élève (l'étudiant)

l'élève (l'étudiante)

le livre

le cahier

le dictionnaire

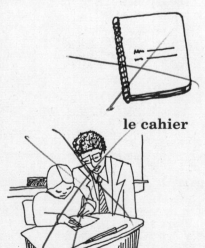

la leçon

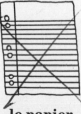

le papier

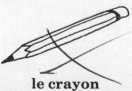

le crayon

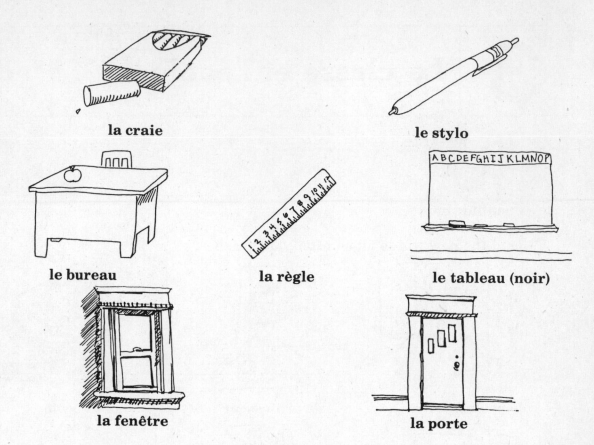

la craie

le stylo

le bureau

la règle

le tableau (noir)

la fenêtre

la porte

Activités

A. Identifiez. Qu'est-ce que c'est? (*What is it?*):

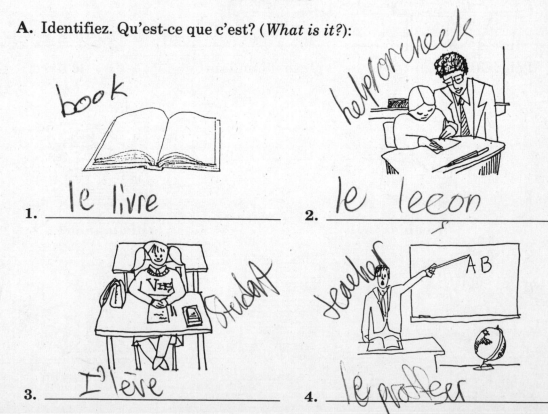

1. le livre

2. le leçon

3. l'élève

4. le profser

kid

dictonary

5. le dictonaire

6. l'élève

notebook

7. le cahièr

8. l'colé

9. le proffeseur

10.

11.

le papier

12.

13.

14.

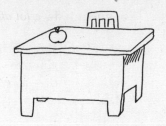

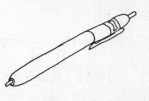

15. _____ 16. _____ le crayon _____

17. _____ 18. _____

B. Fill in the correct definite article **le, la, l'**, or **les:**

1. _____ élève   2. _____ professeur

3. _____ cahier   4. _____ professeurs

5. _____ dictionnaire   6. _____ stylo

7. _____ élèves   8. _____ leçon

9. _____ école   10. _____ tableau

11. _____ porte   12. _____ fenêtre

13. _____ papier   14. _____ bureau

15. _____ règle   16. _____ livre

17. _____ craie   18. _____ crayons

2 Now that you know all of the new words, read the following story and see if you can understand it:

À l'école il y a une classe de français. La classe est intéressante. Le professeur de français est Mme LeFarge. Mme LeFarge est une personne intelligente. En classe, elle emploie un stylo, un crayon, une craie, un tableau noir et un livre de français. Le grand livre est un dictionnaire.

à *at*   **une** *a, an*
de *of*   **français** *French*
Mme (= **madame**) *Mrs.*

emploie *uses*

34

Il y a beaucoup d'élèves dans la classe. Roger est un élève de la classe. Il est populaire parce qu'il est beau. Marie est une élève de la classe. Elle est populaire parce qu'elle est gentille et très intelligente.

beaucoup de *a lot of*   dans *in*

parce que *because*
  beau *handsome*
gentille *nice*   très *very*

Les élèves adorent la classe de français. Le français est une langue populaire et Mme LeFarge est un professeur populaire et sympathique.

langue *language*

sympathique *nice*

Activités

C. Fill in the blanks about the story:

1. La classe de _____ est intéressante.

2. Le professeur est une personne _____.

3. Le professeur de français est _____.

4. Elle emploie _____, _____,

_____, _____.

5. Un dictionnaire est un grand _____.

6. Un élève de la classe est _____.

7. Roger est _____ et _____.

8. Une élève de la classe est _____.

9. Marie est _____ et _____.

10. Les élèves _____ la classe de français.

11. Le français est une langue _____.

12. Mme LeFarge est _____ et _____.

D. OUI ou NON? Correct the wrong answers:

1. Il y a une classe d'**italien**.   _____

2. Le professeur est Mme **Dupont**.   _____

3. Mme LeFarge emploie **un texte**.   _____

4. Roger est **grand**.   _____

5. Marie est **stupide**. _____

6. Le français est **populaire**. _____

E. Form sentences by matching the adjectives with the nouns they describe. Write the answers in the spaces provided:

EXAMPLE: **Le livre/noir** _____ **Le livre est noir.** _____

1. Roger _____ .   grand

2. Mme LeFarge _____ .   gentille

3. Marie _____ .   populaire

4. La classe _____ .   beau

5. Le dictionnaire _____ .   sympathique

6. Le français _____ .   intéressante

3 Now look at the story again. There are two new words that appear many times. What are these two new words? _____ and _____ . These are the words for "a" and "an" in French. See if you can figure out when to use **un** and when to use **une**. Look carefully:

I	II
le tableau noir	*un* tableau noir
le livre	*un* livre
le dictionnaire	*un* dictionnaire
*l'*élève	*un* élève

4 Let's start by comparing the two groups of words. In Group I, are the nouns singular or plural? _____ How do you know? _____

_____ . Are the nouns in Group I masculine or feminine? _____ How do you know? _____

What does **le** mean? _____ Now look at Group II. Are the nouns in Group II singular or plural? _____ What word has replaced **le**? _____ What does **un** mean? _____

5 Let's look at some more examples:

	I	II
	la classe	*une* classe
	la personne	*une* personne
	la règle	*une* règle

In Group I, are the nouns singular or plural? _____ How do you know? _____. Are the nouns in Group I masculine or feminine? _____ How do you know? _____. What does **la** mean? _____

Now look at Group II. Are the nouns singular or plural? _____

What word has replaced **la**? _____ What does **une** mean? _____

6 Let's try one more group:

	I	II
	les livres	*des* livres
	les classes	*des* classes
	les élèves	*des* élèves

In Group I, are the nouns singular or plural? _____ How do you know? _____. Are the nouns in Group I masculine or feminine? _____ Is there any clue to help you figure out the gender of the nouns? _____ What does **les** mean?

_____ Now look at Group II. Are the nouns singular or plural?

_____ What word has replaced **les**? _____ What does

des mean? _____

7 Let's summarize:

_____ is used before masculine singular nouns to express "a" or "an."

_____ is used before feminine singular nouns to express "a" or "an."

_____ is used before masculine and feminine plural nouns to express "some."

Remember, to make most French nouns plural, simply add _____ to the noun.

Activités

F. Match the words with the pictures:

des papiers   des cahiers   des règles
des élèves   une règle   un bureau
un professeur   une porte
une fenêtre   un élève

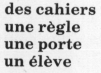

1. _____

2. _____

3. _____

4. _____

5. _____

6. _____

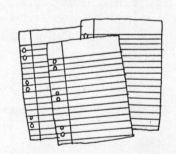

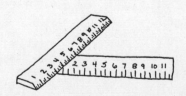

7. _____

8. _____

38

9. _____ **10.** _____

G. Now substitute the word **un, une,** or **des** for **le, la,** or **les:**

1. le chien _____

2. les parents _____

3. le dictionnaire _____

4. la famille _____

5. le tableau _____

6. le professeur _____

7. les papiers _____

8. la craie _____

9. l'étudiante _____

10. l'ami _____

H. Now try some on your own. Fill in **un, une,** or **des:**

1. _____ sœur   2. _____ chat

3. _____ bébés   4. _____ leçon

5. _____ ami   6. _____ frère

7. _____ livre   8. _____ frères

9. _____ étudiant   10. _____ crayon

CONVERSATION

Bonjour, Charles.

Bonjour, madame Dupont.

Où est le livre de français?

Voici le livre, madame.

Bon. Et le crayon?

Voilà le crayon, le stylo et le cahier.

Vous êtes bien préparé, Charles.

Merci, madame Dupont. La classe de français est ma classe favorite.

VOCABULAIRE

où *where*
le livre de français *the French book*
voici *here is, here are*
voilà *there is, there are*
bon *good*

et *and*
vous êtes *you are*
bien *well*
préparé *prepared*

DIALOGUE

What would the first person in this dialog say? Circle your selections from the choices provided:

Bonjour, Paul.
Au revoir, Paul.
À demain, Paul.

Bonjour, M. Lamont.

Comment allez-vous?
Où est la règle?
Comment vous appelez-vous?

Voici la règle,
monsieur.

Et vous?
Et la règle?
Et le stylo?

Voilà le stylo et la
craie.

Vous êtes un monstre, Paul.
Vous êtes très intelligent.
Vous êtes cruel.

Merci, M. Lamont.

QUESTIONS PERSONNELLES

1. Où est le stylo?

_____

2. Où est le tableau noir?

_____

VOUS

The school year is just beginning. You are writing a shopping list of the supplies you will need for the semester. What will you include on your list?

1. _____

2. _____

3. _____

4. _____

5.

6.

7.

8.

1 The new words that follow are all adjectives. They describe the people or objects in the pictures. See if you can guess their meanings:

petit

grand

brun

vert

noir

fort

laid

triste

pauvre

jeune

2 Here is a list of adjectives that are similar to English adjectives. How many meanings can you fill in?

1. africain _____

2. américain _____

3. français _____

4. japonais _____

5. mexicain _____

6. bleu _____

7. blond _____

8. jaune _____

9. rouge _____

10. aimable _____

11. charmant _____

12. confortable _____

13. content _____

14. différent _____

15. dynamique _____

16. élégant _____

17. excellent _____

18. exquis _____

19. fort _____

20. immense _____

21. important _____

22. intelligent _____

23. intéressant _____

24. magnifique _____

25. mince   _____

26. moderne   _____

27. ordinaire   _____

28. parfait   _____

29. pauvre   _____

30. populaire   _____

31. riche   _____

32. sociable   _____

33. splendide   _____

34. stupide   _____

35. superbe   _____

36. surpris   _____

37. timide   _____

3   Now see if you can read and understand these two stories:

Jean est un garçon français. Il est grand et blond. Il est très fort. Il est aussi élégant et charmant. Il étudie le français. Il adore la classe de français. Il est très intelligent, intéressant et populaire. C'est un garçon parfait.

il *he*

étudie *studies*

c'est *he is*

Jeanne est une jeune fille africaine. Elle est petite et brune. Elle est élégante et charmante, surtout quand elle danse. Elle danse très bien. Elle danse les danses américaines et africaines. Elle aussi étudie le français. Elle est intéressante et très intelligente. Elle adore les garçons mais elle est timide. Elle est populaire. C'est une jeune fille parfaite.

elle *she*

surtout *especially*   **quand** *when* **bien** *well*

mais *but*

Activités

A. Make a list from the story of all the adjectives that describe Jean:

1. _____ 2. _____

3. _____ 4. _____

5. _____ 6. _____

7. _____ 8. _____

9. _____ 10. _____

B. Make a list from the story of all the adjectives that describe Jeanne:

1. _____ 2. _____

3. _____ 4. _____

5. _____ 6. _____

7. _____ 8. _____

9. _____ 10. _____

C. Change all of the words in bold type to make the sentences true:

1. Jean est un garçon **africain**. _____

2. Jean est très **faible**. _____

3. Il est **petit** et **brun**. _____

4. Il adore **Jeanne**. _____

5. C'est un garçon **cruel**. _____

6. Jeanne est une jeune fille **américaine**. _____

7. Elle est **blonde** et **immense**. _____

8. Elle **chante** très bien. _____

9. Elle étudie les **mathématiques**. _____

10. Elle adore **le professeur**. _____

4 Have you been observant? Look at the adjectives that could describe Jean. Compare them with the adjectives that could describe Jeanne:

élégant	élégante
charmant	charmante
intelligent	intelligente
intéressant	intéressante
blond	blonde
brun	brune
fort	forte
grand	grande
petit	petite
parfait	parfaite

Adjectives in French agree in gender (sex) with the person or thing they are describing. What letter do we have to add to the MASCULINE form of the

adjective to get the FEMININE form? We add the letter _____.

Activités

D. Choose the adjective that correctly describes the subject:

1. Jean est _____ (fort, forte).

2. Marie est _____ (content, contente).

3. La porte est _____ (bleu, bleue).

4. Le livre est _____ (intéressant, intéressante).

5. Le tableau est _____ (noir, noire).

6. Le papier est _____ (vert, verte).

7. La mère est _____ (charmant, charmante).

8. La famille est _____ (grand, grande).

9. Le professeur est _____ (américain, américaine).

10. La jeune fille est _____ (blond, blonde).

E. Now see if you can fill in the correct adjective with the proper ending:

1. (big)   Le livre est _____.

2. (surprised)   La femme est _____.

3. (important)   La musique est _____.

4. (blond)   Le garçon est _____.

47

5. (French)   La sœur est _____.

6. (excellent)   La classe est _____.

7. (small)   La mère est _____.

8. (exquisite)   Le sandwich est _____.

9. (perfect)   La table est _____.

10. (Mexican)   Marie est _____.

5 Now look at these adjectives that describe Jean and Jeanne:

timide	timide
populaire	populaire
riche	riche
ordinaire	ordinaire
pauvre	pauvre
superbe	superbe
splendide	splendide
magnifique	magnifique
immense	immense
stupide	stupide
mince	mince

What do you notice about the adjectives in both columns? _____

_____ Adjectives in French agree in gender with the person or thing they are describing. For these adjectives, however, we did not add **e** to get the feminine form. Why do you think we did

not have to add **e**? _____

A good rule to remember is: When the masculine form of an adjective ends in

a silent **e,** the feminine form _____.

Activité

F. Complete each sentence with the correct form of the adjective:

1. Le livre est rouge; la table est _____ aussi.

2. Le professeur est riche; l'étudiante est _____ aussi.

3. Le programme est superbe; la classe est _____ aussi.

4. Pierre est timide; Marie est _____ aussi.

5. Le lac est splendide; la rivière est _____ aussi.

6 There is still more to learn about adjectives. See if you can complete the second column:

I	II
élégant	**élégants**
charmant	**charmants**
riche	**riches**
pauvre	**pauvres**
intelligent	_____
intéressant	_____
blond	_____
brun	_____
fort	_____
grand	_____
petit	_____
timide	_____
populaire	_____

Look at Group I. How many people are we describing? _____

Look at Group II. How many people are we describing? _____

What letter did we have to add to the adjective to show that we are describing

more than one person? We added the letter _____.

Adjectives in French agree in GENDER and NUMBER with the person or thing they are describing.

Think carefully. What will be the plural form of the adjective if the singular form already ends in **s**?

EXAMPLES: **Le garçon est surpris.   Les garçons sont** _____.

Le sandwich est exquis.   Les sandwiches sont _____.

49

7 Can you finish Group II?

I	II
élégante	élégantes
charmante	charmantes
intelligente	intelligentes
intéressante	intéressantes

blonde   _____

brune   _____

forte   _____

grande   _____

petite   _____

timide   _____

populaire   _____

riche   _____

pauvre   _____

Look at Group I. What is the gender of the noun we are describing?

_____ What letter did we have to add to get the feminine form?

_____ How many people are we describing in Group I? _____

Look at Group II. How many feminine people are we describing? _____

_____ What extra letter did we have to add to the adjective to show that we are describing more than one feminine person? We

added the letter _____.

Activités

G. Complete the sentences. Add an ending to the adjective if necessary:

1. (moderne)   Les parents sont _____.

2. (surpris)   La jeune fille est _____.

3. (riche)   Le garçon est _____.

4. (intelligent)   Les sœurs sont _____.

5. (bleu)   Les livres sont _____ .

6. (fort)   Les hommes sont _____ .

7. (américain)   Les mères sont _____ .

8. (timide)   L'étudiante est _____ .

9. (exquis)   Les jeunes filles sont _____ .

10. (petit)   La classe est _____ .

H. Match the nouns in the left column with the adjectives in the right column and write your answers in the spaces provided. Pay special attention to the endings:

1. les chats _____ confortable

2. le restaurant _____ intéressant

3. la famille _____ modernes

4. les hôtels _____ populaire

5. la danse _____ bleu

6. le journal _____ aimable

7. le stylo _____ africaine

8. les professeurs _____ grillé

9. l'acteur _____ intelligents

10. le sandwich _____ charmants

I. Complete the sentence with the correct form of the adjective:

1. L'homme est _____ (mexicain, mexicaine, mexicains, mexicaines).

2. Le professeur est _____ (superbe, superbes).

3. Les grandes autos sont _____ (vert, verte, verts, vertes).

4. Le chat est _____ (intelligent, intelligente, intelligents, intelligentes).

5. Les amis sont _____ (riche, riches).

6. Le stylo est _____ (bleu, bleue, bleus, bleues).

7. La famille est _____ (petit, petite, petits, petites).

8. Les monstres sont _____ (grand, grande, grands, grandes).

9. C'est une université _____ (important, importante, importants, importantes).

10. Les voyages sont _____ (intéressant, intéressante, intéressants, intéressantes).

J. Fill in the correct form of the adjective in French:

1. (brown)   La guitare est _____

2. (big)   La cathédrale est _____

3. (comfortable) Les théâtres sont _____

4. (modern)   L'appartement est _____

5. (small)   La photo est _____

6. (content)   Les filles sont _____

7. (blond)   Les garçons sont _____

8. (charming)   La musique est _____

9. (blue)   Les stylos sont _____

8 Carefully read the following phrases:

I	II
Le monstre est fort.	un monstre fort
L'université est moderne.	une université moderne
Le programme est intéressant.	un programme intéressant
Les restaurants sont excellents.	des restaurants excellents
Les livres sont rouges.	des livres rouges

The sentences in Group I all contain a word that is missing from the phrases

in Group II. This word is _____. Is this word a noun, a verb, or an

adjective? _____ Whether or not you have a verb, what is the

position of the adjective in the sentence? _____ Does the

adjective come before or after the noun? _____ In

French, most adjectives come _____ the nouns they modify.

There are some exceptions. Four common adjectives that come before the nouns they modify are:

petit   **grand**   **jeune**   **joli**

EXAMPLES: **un *petit* garçon**   **un *jeune* tigre**
          une *grande* fille   **une *jolie* élève**

Activités

K. Following the examples in Group II, take out the verb to make a new phrase using the adjective:

1. Les roses sont rouges.   _____

2. La famille est riche.   _____

3. Le sandwich est grillé.   _____

4. Les autos sont confortables.   _____

5. Les jeunes filles sont américaines.   _____

6. La mère est blonde.   _____

7. Les danses sont populaires.   _____

8. Le programme est intéressant.   _____

9. L'homme est pauvre.   _____

10. Les chats sont intelligents.   _____

L. Give the noun + adjective that describe each picture.   Follow the first example:

1. un homme triste   2. _____

3. _____

4. _____

5. _____

6. _____

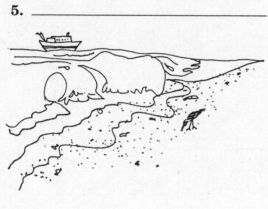

7. _____

8. _____

9. _____

10. _____

CONVERSATION

Pardon, monsieur l'agent. Où est le grand cinéma?

Il y a beaucoup de grands cinémas ici. Vous cherchez le cinéma dans quelle rue?

La rue de Rivoli.

Ah, oui. C'est le cinéma Paris près du petit parc.

Il est loin?

Non. À cinq minutes d'ici.

Merci.

À votre service.

VOCABULAIRE

il y a *there is, there are*
beaucoup de *many*
ici *here*
quelle *which*
la rue *the street*

près du *near the*
loin *far*
cinq *five*
de *from, of*
à votre service *at your service, you're welcome*

DIALOGUE

Fill in the correct responses in the dialog. Choose your responses from the list provided below:

Pardon, madame. Où est le théâtre?

_____

Le théâtre dans l'avenue de l'Opéra.

_____

Il est loin d'ici?

_____

Merci.

_____

Non, il est près d'ici.   À votre service.
Quel théâtre cherchez-vous?   Ah oui. C'est le théâtre près du parc.

QUESTIONS PERSONNELLES

1. Qui est populaire dans la classe?

_____

2. Qui est intelligent(e)?

_____

3. Qui est intéressant(e)?

_____

VOUS

You are the editor of the school yearbook. Fill in the students' names and describe each of them by using three adjectives.

Il est

Ils sont

Elle est

Elles sont

Révision I (Leçons 1-4)

Leçon 1

There are four ways to say "the" in French:

le is used before masculine singular nouns beginning with a consonant.
la is used before feminine singular nouns beginning with a consonant.
l' is used before masculine and feminine singular nouns beginning with a vowel.
les is used before ALL plural nouns.

Leçon 2

To make most French nouns plural, add **s** to the singular form of the noun.

Leçon 3

There are two ways to say "a" or "an" in French. The pural of "a" or "an" is "some":

un is used before masculine singular nouns to express "a" or "an."
une is used before feminine singular nouns to express "a" or "an."
des is used before all plural nouns to express "some."

Leçon 4

Adjectives agree in number and gender with the nouns they modify. For most adjectives, add **e** to the masculine form of the adjective to get the feminine form.

When the masculine form of the adjective already ends in an **e**, no **e** is added to form the feminine adjective.

When the adjective describes a plural noun, add **s** to get the plural form of the adjective.

Activités

A. Identify the pictures in French and then find the French words in the word-search puzzle on page 60:

58

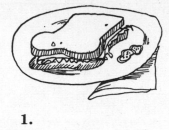

1.

2.

3.

4.

5.

6.

7.

8.

9.

10.

11.

12.

13.

14.

15.

59

```
A R L I V R E P S O
F M A N E I H C P O
L O U B R E F A E L
S I E S T E E R L Y
O B T R I U H O G T
U D O R U Q C T E S
P P L V A S U T R I
E T A H C I L E S A
D H C I W D N A S R
N O I S I V E L E T
```

B. Use an adjective to describe these people or things:

1. Le livre de français est _____.

2. Le professeur est _____.

3. Le directeur de l'école est _____.

4. Les garçons sont _____.

5. Les filles sont _____.

C. How many of these words do you remember? Fill in the French words, then read down the boxed column of letters. You will find the name of everyone's favorite subject:

1. window ___ __ __ __ __ __ __

2. ruler ___ __ __ __ __

3. car ___ __ __ __

4. nation ___ __ __ __ __

5. lesson __ __ ___ __ __

6. tree ___ __ __ __

7. he ___ __

8. sandwich ___ __ __ __ __ __ __ __

60

D. Bureau d'objets trouvés (*Lost and Found*)

You are working in a lost-and-found office. The following objects have been brought in. Make a list of them to be posted.

OBJETS TROUVÉS

1. _____

2. _____

3. _____

4. _____

5. _____

6. _____

7. _____

8. _____

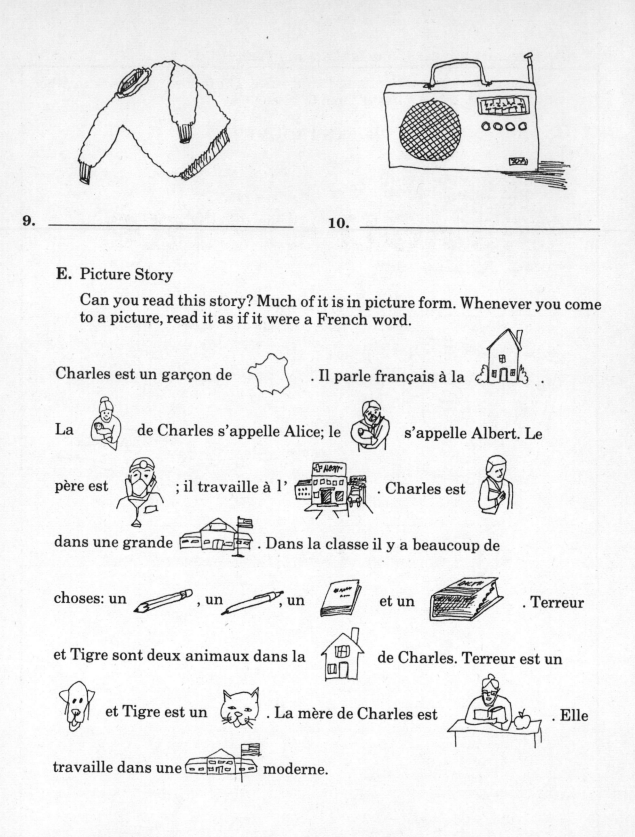

9. _____   10. _____

E. Picture Story

Can you read this story? Much of it is in picture form. Whenever you come to a picture, read it as if it were a French word.

Charles est un garçon de ⬜ . Il parle français à la 🏠 .

La 👤 de Charles s'appelle Alice; le 👤 s'appelle Albert. Le

père est 👨 ; il travaille à l' 🏥 . Charles est

dans une grande 🏫 . Dans la classe il y a beaucoup de

choses: un ✏️ , un 🖊️ , un 📖 et un 📚 . Terreur

et Tigre sont deux animaux dans la 🏠 de Charles. Terreur est un

🐕 et Tigre est un 🐱 . La mère de Charles est 👩‍🏫 . Elle

travaille dans une 🏫 moderne.

VOCABULAIRE

il parle français *he speaks French*	**s'appelle** *is called, (his/her) name is*
à la *at the*	**la chose** *the thing, the object*

62

Deuxième Partie

5 | Les verbes

1 The new words that follow are all verbs. They describe actions. See if you can guess their meanings:

chanter

chercher

danser

donner

écouter

goûter

parler

préparer

regarder

trouver

Activité

A. Match the verb with the noun that could be used with it and write your answers in the spaces provided:

1. goûter _____ la radio

2. chercher _____ la définition

3. regarder _____ français

4. préparer _____ la réponse

5. écouter _____ la télévision

6. chanter _____ disco

7. danser _____ la mousse

8. parler _____ le dîner

9. trouver _____ Frère Jacques

10. donner _____ le dictionnaire

2 Many people will be involved in the story that you are about to read. Who are they?

I	II
je (*I*)	**nous** (*we*)
tu (*you*)	**vous** (*you*)
il (*he*)	**ils** (*they* [*boys; boys and girls*])
elle (*she*)	**elles** (*they* [*girls*])

These words are called subject pronouns. How many people do the subject

pronouns in Group I refer to? _____ How many people do the subject

pronouns in Group II refer to? _____ You will notice that **tu** and **vous**

both mean *you*. When do you use **tu?** _____ When do you use

vous? _____

tu is used when you are speaking to a close relative or a friend, to people with whom you are *familiar*.

vous is used when you are speaking to a person or persons with whom you should be *formal*.

3 What pronoun would you use if you were referring to **Charles?** _____

Marie? _____ **Charles et Paul?** _____ **Marie et Anne?** _____

Marie et Paul? _____ .

Il and **elle** may also mean *it*. Which one would you use to refer to **le livre?**

_____ **la règle?** _____

Ils and **elles** mean *they*. Which one would you use to refer to **les livres?**

_____ **les maisons?** _____

Activités

B. Write the pronoun you would use if you were speaking to:

1. le docteur   _____

2. Roger   _____

3. Marie et Sylvie   _____

4. le professeur   _____

5. la mère   _____

6. le bébé   _____

C. Write the pronoun you could use to substitute for each name or noun:

1. Paul   _____

2. M. Dupont   _____

3. Anne et Denise   _____

4. Monsieur et Madame Dupont _____

5. Suzette   _____

6. les artistes   _____

7. la règle   _____

8. le cahier   _____

9. les stylos   _____

10. les restaurants   _____

4 Now read this story about an interesting French lesson:

Goûtez-vous la mousse au chocolat?

ANNE: **Goûtes-tu** la mousse au chocolat de Mme Navet?

JEAN: Oui, **je goûte** la mousse. Elle est délicieuse. Est-ce que **Claude goûte** la mousse aussi?

ANNE: Oui, **il goûte** la mousse. Et Marie. **Elle goûte** la mousse aussi. Eh, Paul, Roger, **goûtez-vous** la mousse délicieuse?

PAUL ET ROGER: Oui, **nous goûtons** la mousse. (Ils ont le hoquet.)

ils ont le hoquet *they have the hiccups*

ANNE: Mais Madame Navet, ils sont très contents, trop contents. Pourquoi? Ils mangent beaucoup de mousse.

mais *but*
trop *too*
ils mangent *they eat*

MADAME NAVET: Oh là là. Ils mangent trop de mousse. Il y a du cognac dans la mousse. Paul et Roger sont ivres.

trop de *too much*
ivre *drunk*

Activité

D. OUI ou NON? Change the wrong words to correct the sentence:

1. Les élèves goûtent la mousse **à la vanille.** _____

2. La mousse est **horrible.** _____

3. Paul et Roger ont **la fièvre.** _____

4. Paul et Roger sont très **contents.** _____

5. Il y a du **vin** dans la mousse. _____

5 **Goûter** is a verb. It is called an **-ER** verb. All of the verbs in this chapter belong to the **-ER** family because all their infinitives (their basic forms) end in **-ER** and because they all follow the same rules for verb CONJUGATION.

CONJUGATION, what's that? CONJUGATION refers to changing the ending of the verb so that the verb agrees with the subject. We do the same in English without even thinking about it. For example, we say *I taste*, but *he tastes*. Look carefully at the forms of the verb **goûter** in bold type in the story and see if you can answer these questions.

a. To conjugate the verb (to make the subject and verb agree) what letters

are dropped from the infinitive **goûter?** _____

b. What ending do we add to this stem for the following subject pronouns?

je goût_____   nous goût_____

tu goût_____   vous goût_____

il goût_____   ils goût_____

elle goût_____   elles goût_____

Il can be replaced by the name of a _____.

Elle can be replaced by the name of a _____.

Ils can be replaced by the names of _____.

Elles can be replaced by the names of _____.

These rules are true for most **-ER** verbs. There are a few exceptions that you
will meet in later lessons.

NOTE: **J'écoute la musique.**
What happened to the **e** in **je?** _____

What did we put in place of the **e** in **je?** _____

Why did we do this? _____

There are three possible meanings for each verb phrase:

EXAMPLE: **je goûte** *I taste*   **tu goûtes** *you taste*
                        I do taste   *you do taste*
                        I am tasting   *you are tasting*

              il goûte *he tastes*   **elle goûte** *she tastes*
                            he does taste   *she does taste*
                            he is tasting   *she is tasting*

Now fill in the three possible meanings:

nous goûtons   1. _____

                   2. _____

                   3. _____

vous goûtez   1. _____

                   2. _____

                   3. _____

ils goûtent   1. _____

2. _____

3. _____

elles goûtent   1. _____

2. _____

3. _____

NOTE: We do not express *do, does, am, are, is* in French because these words are included in the meaning of the French verb.

Activités

E. Can you conjugate these **-er** verbs?

	chanter	**danser**	**regarder**	**parler**
je	_____	_____	_____	_____
tu	_____	_____	_____	_____
il	_____	_____	_____	_____
elle	_____	_____	_____	_____
nous	_____	_____	_____	_____
vous	_____	_____	_____	_____
ils	_____	_____	_____	_____
elles	_____	_____	_____	_____

F. Match the descriptions with the correct pictures:

Je goûte la mousse. Elles parlent.
Nous chantons. Ils préparent la mousse.
Ils dansent. Tu donnes le livre à Paul.
Elle regarde la télévision. Vous regardez le tableau.
Vous écoutez la musique. Il trouve le livre.

1. _____

2. _____

3. _____

4. _____

5. _____

6. _____

7. _____

8. _____

9. _____   10. _____

G. Here are ten verb forms in French. Fill in a correct subject pronoun:
EXAMPLES: **je parle/il parle/elle parle**

1. _____ goûtons   6. _____ préparez

2. _____ parlez   7. _____ regarde

3. _____ dansent   8. _____ donnons

4. _____ chantes   9. _____ trouve

5. _____ écoute   10. _____ cherches

H. Fill in the correct forms of the verbs. Be sure to drop all the **-er** endings before starting:

1. (goûter) Je _____

2. (parler) Tu _____

3. (danser) Il _____

4. (chanter) Elle _____

5. (écouter) Nous _____

6. (préparer) Vous _____

7. (regarder) Ils _____

8. (donner) Elles _____

9. (trouver) Marie _____

10. (parler) Marie et Sylvie _____

11. (danser) Paul _____

12. (chanter) Paul et Roger _____

I. Now make complete French sentences by adding the correct verb form:

1. (tastes)   Elle _____ la mousse.

2. (speak)   Vous _____ italien.

3. (dance)   Nous _____.

4. (sing)   Je _____.

5. (listen)   Ils _____.

6. (prepare)   Tu _____ la salade.

7. (looks at)   Il _____ la petite fille.

8. (give)   Elles _____ une définition.

9. (finds)   Marie _____ le livre.

10. (look for)   Paul et Anne _____ le disque.

J. Write 5 short original sentences in French using **-er** verbs and give three possible meanings for each:

1. _____

_____

_____

_____

2. _____

_____

_____

_____

3. _____

_____

_____

_____

4. _____

_____

_____

_____

5. _____

_____

_____

_____

QUESTIONS PERSONNELLES

1. Dansez-vous bien?

_____

2. Chantez-vous en classe?

_____

3. Qu'est-ce que (*What*) vous regardez?

_____

4. Qui est-ce que (*To whom*) vous écoutez?

_____

5. Parlez-vous français?

_____

CONVERSATION

Bonjour, Docteur Maxime.

Bonjour, Gaston. Où est mon auto?

Ici. Vous désirez l'auto pour demain?

Bien sûr. J'emploie l'auto pour visiter les malades.

Le moteur consomme trop d'essence.

Oh là là. Est-il possible de réparer l'auto tout de suite?

Bien sûr.

Merci, Gaston. À demain.

VOCABULAIRE

mon *my*	**consommer** *to consume*
avoir *to have*	**trop de** *too much*
pour *for*	**l'essence** *the gasoline*
demain *tomorrow*	**est-il** *is it*
bien sûr *of course*	**réparer** *repair*
malade *sick* (person)	**tout de suite** *right away*

DIALOGUE

Fill in the words that are missing in the dialog. Choose from the list provided below:

_____, docteur Maxime.

    Bonjour, Gaston. Où est _____?

Ici. _____-vous l'auto pour demain?

    J'emploie l'auto pour _____ les

    _____ malades.

Le _____ consomme trop d'essence.

    Oh là là. Est-il _____ de réparer vite l'auto?

Oui, bien _____.

    Au _____, Gaston. À _____.

désirez	personnes	possible
bonjour	sûr	moteur
visiter	ma voiture	demain
revoir		

VOUS

List four things you do from the time you get home from school until dinner is ready:

1. _____

2. _____

3. _____

4. _____

6 | Encore des verbes

1 Here are **-ER** verbs. Can you guess their meanings?

aimer

arriver

demander

entrer

fermer

gagner

habiter

inviter

jouer

marcher

penser

travailler

77

Activité

A. Fill in the correct form of a verb that makes sense in the sentences:

1. Philippe _____ Julie.

2. Nous _____ à l'école.

3. J' _____ dans la classe.

4. Vous _____ une grande maison.

5. Ils _____ le match de football.

6. Marie _____ dans le parc.

7. Le professeur _____ la porte.

8. Elles _____ les garçons à la surprise-partie.

9. Pierre _____ que Sylvie est populaire.

10. Le docteur _____ à l'hôpital.

2 Now look at these sentences:

I	II
Hubert danse.	Hubert *ne* danse *pas*.
Régine joue.	Régine *ne* joue *pas*.
Je marche.	Je *ne* marche *pas*.
Il entre.	Il *n'*entre *pas*.

How are the sentences in Group I different in meaning from the sentences in

Group II? _____

_____

What two little words are used in French to make the sentences negative?

_____ Where do we put **ne** in relation to the verb?

_____

Where do we put **pas?** _____ Look at the

last sentence. What happened to the e in **ne?** _____ What

did we put in its place? _____ Why did we do so?

_____

Let's see what the sentences in Group II above mean in English. Each sentence has two meanings. What are they?

1. _____

_____

2. _____

_____

3. _____

_____

4. _____

_____

What words do we use in English that are not used in French?

_____

We do not use *do, does, is, am, are* in French because these words are included in the meaning of the French verb.

EXAMPLE: **Je marche.** *I walk. I do walk. I am walking.*
Je *ne* marche *pas*. *I do not walk. I am not walking.*

Activité

B. Make the following sentences negative:

1. Paul danse. _____

2. Les petites filles chantent. _____

3. Il imite un animal. _____

4. J'adore le professeur. _____

5. Elles préparent le dîner. _____

6. Nous écoutons la radio. _____

7. Vous travaillez beaucoup. _____

8. Tu demandes le sandwich. _____

9. Ils arrivent. _____

10. Elle invite les garçons. _____

79

11. J'habite la maison bleue. _____

12. Vous marchez dans le parc. _____

13. Tu cherches le dictionnaire. _____

14. Nous fermons les livres. _____

15. Il entre dans la classe. _____

3 You now know how to make any sentence in French negative. Now let's find out how to ask a question in French:

<table>
<tr><td>I</td><td>II</td></tr>
<tr><td>Je danse.</td><td>EST-CE QUE je danse?</td></tr>
<tr><td>Tu entres.</td><td>EST-CE QUE tu entres?</td></tr>
<tr><td>Il chante.</td><td>EST-CE QU'il chante?</td></tr>
<tr><td>Nous écoutons.</td><td>EST-CE QUE nous écoutons?</td></tr>
<tr><td>Vous travaillez.</td><td>EST-CE QUE vous travaillez?</td></tr>
<tr><td>Elles marchent.</td><td>EST-CE QU'elles marchent?</td></tr>
</table>

What did we add to all the statements in Group I to form the questions in

Group II? _____

What happens to the e in **que** before **il, ils, elle, elles?** _____

_____

Why is the e of **que** dropped?_____

Let's see what the sentences in Group II above mean in English:

1. _____

2. _____

3. _____

4. _____

5. _____

6. _____

What words do we use in English that are not used in French?

_____

We do not use *do, does, is, am, are* in French because these words are included in the meaning of the French verb.

Activité

C. Change the following statements to questions and tell what they mean in English:

1. Le docteur arrive. _____

   _____

2. La guitare est magnifique. _____

   _____

3. Je prépare le dîner. _____

   _____

4. Vous préparez les devoirs. _____

   _____

5. Nous écoutons le professeur. _____

   _____

6. Tu fermes le livre. _____

   _____

7. Ils pensent en classe. _____

   _____

8. Elle travaille à l'hôpital. _____

   _____

9. Elles habitent un appartement. _____

   _____

10. Les garçons parlent français. _____

    _____

11. Il aime la jeune fille. _____

    _____

12. Les enfants jouent à la maison. _____

    _____

4 There is another way to form a question in French. Observe these sentences:

Tu parles.	Parles-tu?
Nous chantons.	Chantons-nous?
Vous dansez bien.	Dansez-vous bien?
Ils écoutent la musique.	Écoutent-ils la musique?
Elles gagnent le match.	Gagnent-elles le match?

This way of forming a question is called inversion because we invert, that is, we change the word order. Look carefully and tell how the word order is

changed: _____

Activité

D. Change these sentences to questions by changing the order of the subject and verb. Give the meanings of the questions you write:

1. Tu gagnes la compétition. _____

   _____

2. Vous aimez le disque. _____

   _____

3. Nous jouons en classe. _____

   _____

4. Ils cherchent le parc. _____

   _____

5. Elles arrivent à la maison. _____

   _____

6. Tu invites les filles. _____

   _____

7. Ils travaillent beaucoup. _____

   _____

8. Nous habitons à New York. _____

   _____

9. Vous demandez un crayon. _____

_____

10. Elles pensent en français. _____

_____

5 Which subject pronoun does not occur in these sentences? _____ Note the following:

a. We do not usually invert with **je.** If you can't invert with **je,** how will you

form a question if the subject is **je?** _____

b. Look carefully:

Il danse	**Danse-_t_-il?**
Elle travaille.	**Travaille-_t_-elle?**
Il parle.	**Parle-_t_-il?**
Elle chante.	**Chante-_t_-elle?**

Did we invert with **il** and **elle?** _____ But we added an extra letter.

What letter did we add? _____ Where did we put it? _____

_____ How did we join the extra letter to the rest of the question?

_____ Why did we do this? _____
Why don't we have to add the extra letter when **ils** or **elles** is the subject?

_____

Why don't we have to do this when **nous, vous,** or **tu** is the subject? _____

_____

Activité

E. Change these sentences to questions using inversion:

1. Il joue. _____

2. Elle marche. _____

3. Il pense en français. _____

4. Elle habite la maison. _____

5. Il donne le livre à Paul. _____

6. Elle regarde la liste. _____

7. Il aime le bébé. _____

8. Elle cherche la radio. _____

6 There is still one more group of sentences to look at:

Marie danse.	Marie danse-*t-elle*?
Paul parle.	Paul parle-*t-il*?
Marie et Anne chantent.	Marie et Anne chantent-*elles*?
Les garçons regardent le match.	Les garçons regardent-*ils* le match?
Anne et Paul écoutent les disques.	Anne et Paul écoutent-*ils* les disques?
Les livres sont sur la table.	Les livres sont-*ils* sur la table?

Can we form a question by inverting with a person's name or with a noun?

_____ How do we form a question using inversion if the subject is

someone's name or refers to someone or something? _____

_____

> The rule is: In French, we can form a question using inversion only by inverting (changing the word order of) a PRONOUN (**tu, il, elle, nous, vous, ils, elles**) and a VERB.

Activité

F. Change these sentences to questions using inversion:

1. La petite fille arrive. _____

2. Marie écoute. _____

3. Les garçons parlent. _____

4. Paul et Anne dansent beaucoup. _____

5. Les parents aiment le bébé. _____

6. Les maisons sont bleues. _____

7. Les professeurs chantent. _____

8. Les disques sont sur la table. _____

84

9. Le dîner est délicieux. _____

10. La robe est verte. _____

7 Can you understand this interview with an interesting teacher?

ROBERT: Mme Bernard, quelle sorte de musique aimez-vous?

quelle _what_

MME BERNARD: J'aime beaucoup le rock et le disco.

ROBERT: Quel est votre groupe favori de chanteurs?

chanteurs _singers_

MME BERNARD: J'adore les Rolling Stones.

ROBERT: Chantez-vous les chansons des Rolling Stones?

les chansons _the songs_

MME BERNARD: Non, je ne chante pas les chansons des Rolling Stones parce que je ne chante pas bien.

ROBERT: Dansez-vous?

MME BERNARD: Oui, je danse bien mais mon mari ne danse pas. Il a deux pieds gauches. Alors je danse avec les autres.

mon mari _my husband_
les pieds _the feet_
gauche _left_   **autres** _others_

ROBERT: Quels programmes regardez-vous à la télévision?

MME BERNARD: Je regarde tous les feuilletons mélodramatiques.

tous _all_   **les feuilletons mélodramatiques** _the soap operas_

ROBERT: Préparez-vous le dîner?

MME BERNARD: Non, mon mari prépare le dîner.

ROBERT: Mangez-vous le dîner?

MME BERNARD: Oui. Le dîner est toujours délicieux.

ROBERT: Aimez-vous la classe de français?

MME BERNARD: J'adore la classe de français.

Activités

G. Répondez aux questions:

1. Quelle musique Mme Bernard aime-t-elle?

_____

2. Chante-t-elle les chansons des Rolling Stones?

_____

3. Chante-t-elle bien?

_____

4. Danse-t-elle?

_____

5. Qui ne danse pas?

_____

6. Quels programmes Mme Bernard regarde-t-elle?

_____

7. Prépare-t-elle le dîner?

_____

8. Qui prépare le dîner?

_____

9. Mange-t-elle le dîner?

_____

10. Aime-t-elle la classe?

_____

H. Answer these questions about yourself:

1. Quel programme regardez-vous?

_____

2. Chantez-vous bien?

_____

3. Chantez-vous en français?

_____

4. Parlez-vous italien?

_____

5. Écoutez-vous la radio?

   _____

6. Aimez-vous la classe de français?

   _____

7. Préparez-vous le dîner?

   _____

8. Mangez-vous le dîner?

   _____

I. Write five questions that you would like to ask your teacher:

   1. _____

   2. _____

   3. _____

   4. _____

   5. _____

J. Write five questions that you would like to ask a boy or girl in the class:

   1. _____

   2. _____

   3. _____

   4. _____

   5. _____

CONVERSATION

Salut, Rose. Ça va?

Ça va, François, et toi?

Comme ci comme ça. Tu travailles beaucoup dans la classe de français?

Bien sûr, et nous parlons français tous les jours.

Bon. Il est nécessaire de pratiquer beaucoup.

Oui. Maintenant les élèves entrent dans la classe. Au revoir.

Au revoir, Rose.

À tout à l'heure.

VOCABULAIRE

salut *hi!*
ça va? *how's it going?*
ça va *everything's fine, O.K.*
et toi *and you*
comme ci comme ça *so-so*
beaucoup *much, a lot*

dans *in*
tous les jours *every day*
pratiquer *to practice*
maintenant *now*
à tout à l'heure *see you later*

DIALOGUE

Fill in what the first person in this dialog would say. Choose from the list provided below:

_____

Ça va, Gisèle, et toi?

_____

Oui, Je parle français tous les jours.

_____

Oui. Maintenant les élèves entrent dans la classe. Au revoir.

_____

À tout à l'heure.

Ça va bien. Parles-tu français en classe?
Au revoir, André. À demain.
Salut, André. Ça va?
Il est nécessaire de travailler et de pratiquer.

VOUS

Félicitations! Congratulations. You have been chosen the most popular student in your class. You are being interviewed by a reporter for the school newspaper. Tell him 5 things that account for you popularity and success. You might want to use some of these verbs: **danser, chanter, écouter, travailler, parler**

1. _____

2. _____

3. _____

4. _____

5. _____

7   Un, deux, trois . . .

1   How to count in French:

1	un, une	11	onze	21	vingt et un
2	deux	12	douze	22	vingt-deux
3	trois	13	treize		
4	quatre	14	quatorze		
5	cinq	15	quinze	25	vingt-cinq
6	six	16	seize		
7	sept	17	dix-sept		
8	huit	18	dix-huit		
9	neuf	19	dix-neuf		
10	dix	20	vingt	30	trente

Activités

A. Match the French number with the numeral and write it in the space provided:

1. trois   _____ 14

2. quatorze   _____ 20

3. sept   _____ 11

4. dix   _____ 8

5. vingt   _____ 1

6. vingt et un   _____ 21

7. huit   _____ 5

8. seize   _____ 12

9. un   _____ 3

10. cinq   _____ 16

11. quinze   _____ 2

12. deux   _____ 10

13. douze   _____ 15

14. dix-neuf   _____ 7

15. onze   _____ 19

B. Write these numbers in French:

7 _____

11 _____

12 _____

29 _____

26 _____

15 _____

2 _____

16 _____

33 _____

21 _____

14 _____

13 _____

18 _____

4 _____

3 _____

2 Enjoy this story and then answer the questions about it:

Je travaille à la Banque Nationale de Paris. Regardez. Un voleur, Pierre LaTour, désire beaucoup de dollars. Il adore l'argent. Il cherche l'argent. Il trouve l'argent. Il regarde l'argent. Il parle. Il dit: «Donnez-moi de l'argent.» Il est content. Il compte l'argent. Mais, attention, les agents de police arrivent. Ils questionnent Pierre. Pierre dit: «J'adore l'argent. Je demande de l'argent. Je compte l'argent.» Les agents passent les menottes à Pierre. Pierre n'est pas content. Il donne l'argent aux agents.

la banque *the bank*
un voleur *a robber*
l'argent *(the) money*

il dit *he says*
de l'argent *some money*
  il compte *he counts*

passer les menottes *put on handcuffs*

Activités

C. Répondez aux questions:

   1. Qui est Pierre LaTour?

   _____

   2. Que désire-t-il?

   _____

   3. Qu'adore-t-il?

   _____

   4. Que dit-il?

   _____

   5. Que compte-t-il?

   _____

   6. Qui arrive?

   _____

   7. Pourquoi Pierre n'est-il pas content?

   _____

   8. Que donne-t-il aux agents?

   _____

D. Write in French the amount of money Pierre wanted:

   1. $16 _____

   2. $37 _____

   3. $24 _____

   4. $12 _____

   5. $9 _____

   6. $2 _____

   7. $15 _____

8. $26 _____

9. $17 _____

10. $14 _____

11. $29 _____

12. $13 _____

E. The operator would like you to repeat some numbers in French:

Madame, donnez-moi le numéro s'il vous plaît:

1. 456-3278 quatre-cinq-six-trois-deux-sept-huit

2. 879-4621 _____

3. 737-3456 _____

4. 455-6743 _____

5. 620-2987 _____

6. 080-2539 _____

7. 435-8723 _____

F. Your teacher will read some numbers to you. Write the numerals for the number you hear:

EXAMPLE: You hear: **vingt**. You write: **20**

1. _____ 2. _____ 3. _____

4. _____ 5. _____ 6. _____

7. _____ 8. _____

9. _____ 10. _____

G. You will hear a number in English. Write the number in French:

1. _____ 2. _____

3. _____ 4. _____

5. _____ 6. _____

7. _____   **8.** _____

9. _____   **10.** _____

3 Now that you know the numbers from 1-30, let's try some math. First you must memorize the following expressions:

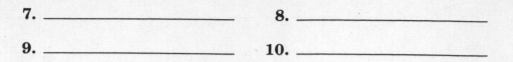

et	_plus (and)_	**divisé par**	_divided by_
moins	_minus (less)_	**font**	_are_
fois	_times_		

EXAMPLES: $2 + 2 = 4$ **deux et deux font quatre**

$5 - 4 = 1$ **cinq moins quatre font un**

$3 \times 3 = 9$ **trois fois trois font neuf**

$12 \div 2 = 6$ **douze divisé par deux font six**

Activités

H. Read the following examples in French. One of them is wrong. Find it and correct it. Write out each problem in numerals:

1. Cinq et cinq font dix.   _____

2. Vingt moins cinq font quinze.   _____

3. Neuf fois deux font dix-huit.   _____

4. Quatre divisé par deux font deux.   _____

5. Six et trois font neuf.   _____

6. Dix-sept moins seize font un.   _____

7. Onze fois un font onze.   _____

8. Vingt divisé par cinq font quatre.   _____

9. Dix-huit divisé par deux font huit.   _____

10. Dix et six font seize.   _____

I. Read the following examples in French and then write them in French:

1. $2 + 3 = 5$ _____

2. $9 - 2 = 7$ _____

3. $4 \times 4 = 16$ _____

4. $8 \div 2 = 4$ _____

5. $12 + 3 = 15$ _____

6. $30 - 5 = 25$ _____

7. $6 \times 5 = 30$ _____

8. $36 \div 3 = 12$ _____

9. $10 + 13 = 23$ _____

10. $12 - 7 = 5$ _____

J. Pick out the correct answer and read it in French. Write out the answer in numerals:

    1. quatre moins deux font _____
        (a) 2 (b) 4 (c) 6 (d) 8

    2. Huit et trois font _____
        (a) 12 (b) 11 (c) 10 (d) 9

    3. Seize divisé par deux font _____
        (a) 3 (b) 12 (c) 9 (d) 8

    4. Deux fois sept font _____
        (a) 4 (b) 14 (c) 21 (d) 36

    5. Quinze et quatorze font _____
        (a) 29 (b) 39 (c) 19 (d) 9

    6. Treize moins deux font _____
        (a) 1 (b) 11 (c) 15 (d) 12

    7. Cinq fois sept font _____
        (a) 25 (b) 35 (c) 15 (d) 12

    8. Trente-deux divisé par huit font _____
        (a) 38 (b) 24 (c) 16 (d) 4

    9. Six et sept font _____
        (a) 3 (b) 23 (c) 13 (d) 33

    10. Vingt moins douze font _____
        (a) 18 (b) 32 (c) 8 (d) 14

K. Complete in French:

    1. Treize et sept font _____

2. Trente-deux moins onze font _____

3. Quatre fois six font _____

4. Quinze divisé par cinq font _____

5. Dix et six font _____

6. Vingt-neuf moins dix-sept font _____

7. Vingt moins douze font _____

8. Sept fois trois font _____

9. Seize moins douze font _____

10. Vingt et dix font _____

QUESTIONS PERSONNELLES

1. Combien (*How many*) de disques écoutez-vous?

_____

2. Combien de programmes regardez-vous?

_____

VOUS

Complete the following information about yourself in French. Write out all numbers:

1. Âge: _____ ans.

2. Nombre de frères: _____ frères.

3. Nombre de sœurs: _____ sœurs.

4. Nombre de membres de la famille: _____ membres.

5. Numéro de téléphone: _____

6. Adresse: _____ rue _____

_____ avenue _____

_____ boulevard _____

8 | Les verbes continuent

1 The new words that follow are all verbs. They belong to the **-IR** family. See if you can guess their meanings:

applaudir

choisir

finir

punir

remplir

saisir

Here are 6 more action words (verbs). You have probably noticed, however, that they do not belong to the **-ER** family. To what family do these verbs

belong? _____ Just as we made changes in the **-ER** verbs by dropping the **-ER** and adding certain endings, we must do the same thing with these verbs. The endings will be different. Let's see what happens. Read the story, look for the **-IR** verbs and see if you can spot the endings.

PIERRE ET JEAN: **Tu finis** les devoirs?
CLAUDE: Oui, **je finis** les devoirs. Pourquoi?   **pourquoi** *why*
PIERRE ET JEAN: Il y a une surprise-partie
   chez Anne.   **chez** *at the house of*
CLAUDE: Quand est-ce que **vous finissez** les   **quand** *when*
   devoirs?

97

PIERRE ET JEAN: **Nous finissons** les devoirs
tout de suite. Allons chez Anne.

CLAUDE: Est-ce que Sylvie va à la surprise-
partie? Elle est magnifique.

PIERRE ET JEAN: Oui, mais d'abord **elle finit**
les devoirs.

CLAUDE: Et Marie et Nadine? Elles sont
élégantes et populaires.

PIERRE ET JEAN: Oui, **elles finissent** les
devoirs maintenant. Elles vont chez Anne
avec nous.

CLAUDE: Allons chez Anne tout de suite.

tout de suite *immediately*

va *goes*

d'abord *first*

maintenant *now*   **vont** *go*

allons *let's go*

Activité

A. Oui ou Non? If the sentence is incorrect, rewrite it correctly:

1. Claude, Jean et Pierre finissent les livres.

   _____

2. La surprise-partie est chez Marie.

   _____

3. Sylvie est stupide.

   _____

4. Marie et Nadine sont charmantes et intelligentes.

   _____

5. Sylvie, Marie et Nadine finissent les devoirs.

   _____

2 Now see if you can complete the correct endings by looking at the story. To
form the present tense of **-IR** verbs: Take the infinitive, drop _____ and
add the endings:

je fin_____   nous fin_____

tu fin_____   vous fin_____

il fin_____   ils fin_____

elle fin_____   elles fin_____

NOTE: **j'applaudis.** What happened to the **e** in **je?** _____

What did we put in place of **e?** _____

Why do we do this? _____

Activités

B. Now let's practice with the other **-ir** verbs:

	applaudir	saisir	punir	choisir	remplir
je	_____	_____	_____	_____	_____
tu	_____	_____	_____	_____	_____
il	_____	_____	_____	_____	_____
elle	_____	_____	_____	_____	_____
nous	_____	_____	_____	_____	_____
vous	_____	_____	_____	_____	_____
ils	_____	_____	_____	_____	_____
elles	_____	_____	_____	_____	_____

C. Fill in the correct subject pronoun:

1. _____ finissez

2. _____ choisissons

3. _____ saisis

4. _____ applaudit

5. _____ punissent

6. _____ remplit

7. _____ saisissons

8. _____ choisis

9. _____ applaudissez

99

10. _____ remplis

11. _____ punit

12. _____ finissent

D. Fill in the correct forms of the verbs. Be sure to drop all the **-ir** endings before starting:

1. (applaudir) Je _____ les acteurs.

2. (saisir) Nous _____ le monstre.

3. (punir) Tu _____ le criminel.

4. (choisir) Vous _____ la classe de français.

5. (finir) Il _____ la leçon.

6. (remplir) Elles _____ les pages.

7. (saisir) Marie _____ le petit enfant.

8. (punir) Paul et Alain _____ l'employé.

9. (choisir) Sylvie et Régine _____ un exercice.

10. (finir) Ils _____ la chanson.

11. (applaudir) Elle _____ le jeune artiste.

12. (remplir) Je _____ le cahier.

13. (applaudir) Nous _____ la musique moderne.

14. (saisir) Je _____ l'occasion.

15. (punir) Vous _____ la classe innocente.

16. (choisir) Tu _____ le verbe correct.

17. (finir) Nous _____ les devoirs.

18. (remplir) Vous _____ la liste.

E. Now make complete French sentences by putting in the correct verb form and an ending to the sentence.

1. (applaud) Tu _____

2. (choose) Nous _____

3. (finish) Je _____

4. (seize) Elles _____

5. (punishes) Anne _____

6. (fills) Il _____

7. (applaud) Vous _____

8. (choose) Je _____

9. (finish) Vous _____

10. (seize) Il _____

11. (punish) Nous _____

12. (fill) Tu _____

F. Match the sentences with the pictures they describe:

Le garçon remplit le verre.
J'applaudis.
Le chef saisit la poule.

La mère punit les enfants.
Elle choisit la réponse correcte.
Il finit le dîner.

1. _____   2. _____

3. _____   4. _____

5. _____   6. _____

QUESTIONS PERSONNELLES

1. Choisissez-vous la réponse correcte?

_____

2. Finissez-vous l'exercice?

_____

3. Applaudissez-vous le professeur dans la classe de français?

_____

VOUS

Write sentences giving information about yourself:

EXAMPLE: **J'applaudis**   **J'applaudis en classe.**

1. J'applaudis   _____

2. Je choisis   _____

3. Je finis   _____

4. Je punis   _____

5. Je remplis   _____

Révision II (Leçons 5-8)

Leçon 5

a. The subject pronouns are:

je (*I*)	**nous** (*we*)
tu (*you*)	**vous** (*you*)
il (*he*)	**ils** (*they*)
elle (*she*)	**elles** (*they*)

b. In order to have a correct verb form with each subject, the verb must be conjugated. Conjugating the verb means changing the original form of the verb so that it agrees with the subject pronoun or noun.

c. In French, there are three verb families: **-ER, -IR, -RE.** All verbs in a specific family follow the same rules of conjugation. Verbs that do not belong to these families or do not follow these rules are called irregular verbs. You have so far met the **-ER** and **-IR** verb families. You will meet the **-RE** family in Leçon 10.

d. The first and largest family consists of **-ER** verbs. To conjugate an **-ER** verb, drop **-ER** from the infinitive (the form of the verb before conjugation):

EXAMPLE: **parler**

If the subject is		add		to the remaining stem:	
	je	add	**e**	to the remaining stem:	**je parle**
	tu		**es**		**tu parles**
	il		**e**		**il parle**
	elle		**e**		**elle parle**
	nous		**ons**		**nous parlons**
	vous		**ez**		**vous parlez**
	ils		**ent**		**ils parlent**
	elles		**ent**		**elles parlent**

Leçon 6

a. To make a sentence negative, that is, to say that a subject does NOT do something, use **ne** and **pas.** Put **ne** before the verb (the action word) and **pas** after the verb:

Je ne parle pas

b. To ask a question, use one of two ways:

Put **est-ce que** at the beginning of the sentence:

Est-ce que je parle?

Put **est-ce qu'** before a vowel (**il** or **elle**):

*Est-ce qu'***il parle?**

OR

Invert (change the order of the subject and verb). Put the verb first, followed by the subject pronoun (do not invert with a noun):

Parlons-nous?

When there is inversion with **il** or **elle**, **-t-** must be put between the verb and the subject. (Do not invert with **je**):

Parle-*t***-il?**
Parle-*t***-elle?**

Leçon 7

1	un	11	onze	21	vingt et un
2	deux	12	douze	22	vingt-deux
3	trois	13	treize	23	vingt-trois
4	quatre	14	quatorze	24	vingt-quatre
5	cinq	15	quinze	25	vingt-cinq
6	six	16	seize	26	vingt-six
7	sept	17	dix-sept	27	vingt-sept
8	huit	18	dix-huit	28	vingt-huit
9	neuf	19	dix-neuf	29	vingt-neuf
10	dix	20	vingt	30	trente

$+$ **et** $-$ **moins** $\times$ **fois** $\div$ **divisé par**

Leçon 8

To conjugate verbs that belong to the **-IR** family, drop **-IR** from the infinitive:

EXAMPLE: **finir**

If the subject is		add		to the remaining stem:	
	je		is		je fin*is*
	tu		is		tu fin*is*
	il		it		il fin*it*
	elle		it		elle fin*it*
	nous		issons		nous fin*issons*
	vous		issez		vous fin*issez*
	ils		issent		ils fin*issent*
	elles		issent		elles fin*issent*

The same rules as for **-ER** verbs apply to making a sentence negative or asking a question, except that no **-t-** is needed for inversion with **il** or **elle**.

Activités

A. Write the French word next to the English word. Then find the French word in the puzzle:

to taste _____

to find _____

to look for _____

to give _____

to sing _____

to fill _____

to punish _____

to choose _____

to finish _____

13 _____

20 _____

16 _____

11 _____

9 _____

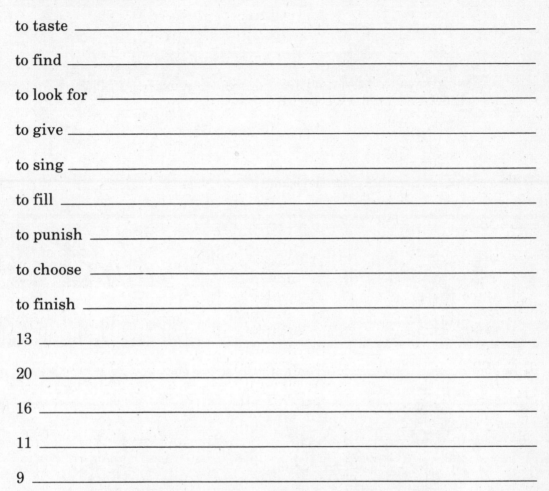

P	U	R	I	L	P	M	E	R	O
R	N	F	C	H	A	N	T	E	R
I	R	A	P	X	I	T	Z	N	N
F	I	N	I	R	R	I	O	R	U
R	S	F	D	E	E	N	Z	I	N
I	I	U	O	S	Z	T	A	E	V
N	O	Z	N	E	N	I	U	D	I
U	H	R	N	P	I	F	E	O	N
P	C	H	E	R	C	H	E	R	G
D	C	O	R	E	V	U	O	R	T

B. Verb Game. Here are some pictures of people doing things. Describe each picture using the correct form of one of the following verbs: **regarder, chanter, punir, préparer, remplir, écouter, applaudir, choisir:**

1. Ils _____ la télévision.

2. Nous _____ Frère Jacques.

3. Le père _____ l'enfant.

4. Les élèves _____ le prof.

5. Maman _____ le dîner.

6. Vous _____ le verre.

7. Jean _____ le disque.

8. Elles _____.

106

C. Mots Croisés.

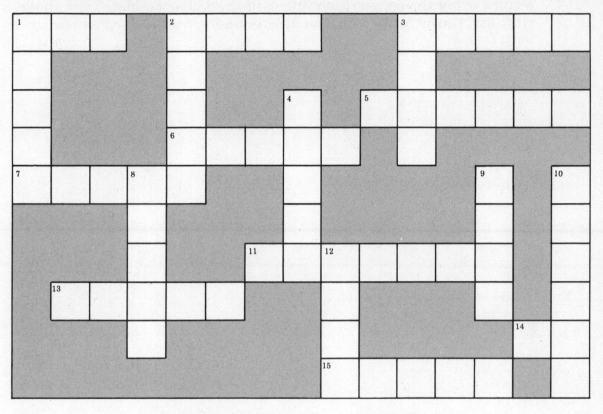

HORIZONTALEMENT	VERTICALEMENT
1. wine	**1.** 20
2. car	**2.** tree
3. dog	**3.** cat
5. notebook	**4.** pupil
6. ruler	**8.** book
7. table	**9.** chef
11. window	**10.** record
13. door	**12.** 9
14. you	
15. girl	

D. Are you a good detective? The police are looking for some missing persons. You have been called in to identify certain snapshots. Match the photos with descriptions. The one who doesn't fit the descriptions has already been found:

1. **Philippe:** 20 ans, laid, brun, timide, expression stupide.

2. **Yvette:** 35 ans, élégante, mince, petite, expression intelligente, triste.

3. **Raoul:** 50 ans, pauvre, petit, expression confuse.

4. **Lisette:** 19 ans, grande, brune, riche, expression cruelle.

5. **Personne trouvée:**

Description: _____

_____

_____

E. All of the following people are saying some numbers. What are they?

1. _____

2. _____

3. _____

4. _____

5. _____

6. _____

F. **L'Avenir.** Wouldn't you like to know your future? Follow these simple rules to see what the cards have in store for you. Choose a number between two and eight. Starting in the upper left-hand corner, and moving from left to right, write down all the letters that appear under that number in French:

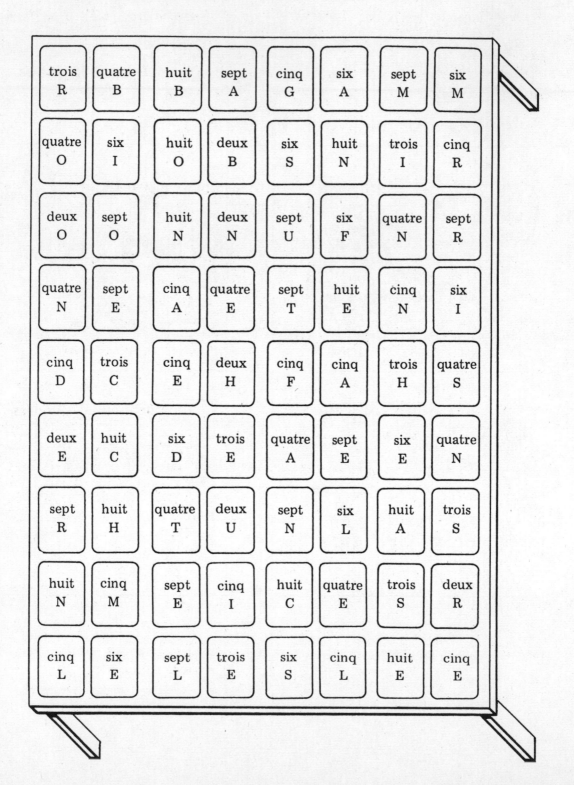

G. Picture Story

Can you read this story? Much of it is in picture form. Whenever you come to a picture, read it as if it were a French word:

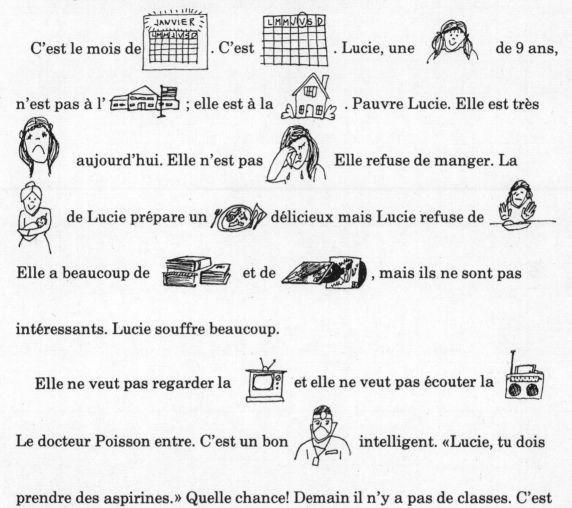

C'est le mois de [janvier]. C'est [vendredi]. Lucie, une [fille] de 9 ans,

n'est pas à l' [école] ; elle est à la [maison]. Pauvre Lucie. Elle est très

[malade] aujourd'hui. Elle n'est pas [contente]. Elle refuse de manger. La

[mère] de Lucie prépare un [repas] délicieux mais Lucie refuse de [manger].

Elle a beaucoup de [livres] et de [journaux], mais ils ne sont pas

intéressants. Lucie souffre beaucoup.

Elle ne veut pas regarder la [télévision] et elle ne veut pas écouter la [radio].

Le docteur Poisson entre. C'est un bon [docteur] intelligent. «Lucie, tu dois

prendre des aspirines.» Quelle chance! Demain il n'y a pas de classes. C'est

[samedi].

VOCABULAIRE

janvier *January*
vendredi *Friday*
journaux *newspapers*
elle ne veut pas *she doesn't want to*

tu dois *you must*
la chance *luck*
samedi *Saturday*

Troisième Partie

1 Vocabulaire

Qui est-ce? C'est

l'acteur

l'actrice

l'agent de police

l'artiste

l'avocat

l'avocate

le dentiste

la dentiste

le docteur, le médecin

le facteur

115

la factrice

l'infirmier

l'infirmière

le pompier

le professeur

le secrétaire

la secrétaire

Activités

A. Match the following occupations with the related pictures:

un professeur	un docteur	une avocate
un agent de police	un acteur	un infirmier
un secrétaire	un pompier	
un dentiste	un facteur	

1. _____   2. _____

3. _____

4. _____

5. _____

6. _____

7. _____

8. _____

9. _____

10. _____

B. Now identify these pictures:

1. _____

2. _____

3. _____

4. _____

5. _____

6. _____

7. _____

8. _____

9. _____

10. _____

2 Look at these sentences for a moment:

Kojak est agent de police.
Mme Dupont est professeur.

What little word did we leave out before the name of the profession? _____

118

Activité

C. Choose eight people you know and write their professions. Write complete sentences:

EXAMPLE: **Trapper John est docteur.**

1. _____

2. _____

3. _____

4. _____

5. _____

6. _____

7. _____

8. _____

3 Read the following story and see if you can answer the questions about it. All of the verb forms in bold type are some form of the verb **être** (*to be*):

JEAN: Est-ce que **Mme Renard,** le professeur de français, **est** sympathique?

ROBERT: Oui, **elle est** sympathique. **Marie et Janine,** les deux filles blondes, **sont** sympathiques, **n'est-ce pas?**

JEAN: Oui, **elles sont** sympathiques. **Ronald est** drôle.

RONALD: Oui, **je suis** drôle, mais **tu es** drôle aussi, Jean.

JEAN ET ROBERT: **Nous sommes** drôles, nous deux. Mais Mme Renard, **vous n'êtes pas** drôle.

MME RENARD: Non, **je ne suis pas** drôle. Mais **je suis** sympathique, dynamique, aimable, sociable et formidable.

n'est-ce pas *isn't that so*

drôle *funny*

nous deux *the two of us*

aimable *friendly*
formidable *terrific*

Activité

D. Répondez aux questions:

1. Qui est sympathique?

_____

2. Comment sont Marie et Janine?

_____

3. Qui est drôle?

_____

4. Qui n'est pas drôle?

_____

5. Comment est Mme Renard?

_____

4 In the story you have just read, there is a new verb. The new verb is **être. Être** is the infinitive of the verb. **Être** means _to be_. **Être** is a special verb because it is one of a kind. No other verb in French is conjugated like **être.** For this reason, **être** is known as an irregular verb. Can you pick out the correct verb form from the story to match the subjects below?

je _____   **nous** _____

tu _____   **vous** _____

il _____   **ils** _____

elle _____   **elles** _____

Since **être** is an irregular verb, how are you going to learn all the forms?

_____

Activités

E. Fill in the correct form of the verb **être:**

1. Je _____ avocat.

2. Elle _____ professeur.

3. Nous _____ drôles.

4. Tu _____ médecin.

5. Ils _____ pompiers.

6. Anne _____ artiste.

7. Vous _____ facteur.

8. Paul et André _____ blonds.

9. Il _____ riche.

10. Elles _____ contentes.

11. Les livres _____ intéressants.

12. Alice et Marie _____ grandes.

F. Make all the sentences in exercise E negative:

1. _____

2. _____

3. _____

4. _____

5. _____

6. _____

7. _____

8. _____

9. _____

10. _____

11. _____

12. _____

G. Change all the sentences in exercise E to questions using inversion. Be careful if the subject is **je** or NOT a pronoun:

1. _____

2. _____

3. _____

4. _____

5. _____

6. _____

7. _____

8. _____

9. _____

10. _____

11. _____

12. _____

H. Fill in the correct subject pronoun:

1. _____ es content.

2. _____ est formidable.

3. _____ sommes secrétaires.

4. _____ suis intelligent.

5. _____ êtes intéressant.

6. _____ sont stupides.

I. Here are some sentences in which a form of **être** is used. Can you match these sentences with the pictures they describe?

Terreur est un chien.　　　　　**Les grands-parents sont âgés.**
Marie et Suzanne sont grandes.　**Nous sommes contents.**
Tu es riche.　　　　　　　　　　**Vous êtes fort.**
Elle est agent de police.　　　　**Je suis fatigué.**

1. _____　　2. _____

3. _____   **4.** _____

5. _____   **6.** _____

7. _____   **8.** _____

QUESTIONS PERSONNELLES

1. Êtes-vous secrétaire? _____

2. Êtes-vous fort(e)? _____

3. Êtes-vous content(e)? _____

4. Comment êtes-vous? _____

VOUS

List in French the 5 professions that interest you most. Next to each profession write a sentence that describes the person involved in that profession:

EXAMPLE: **docteur**   **Le docteur est intelligent.**

1. _____

2. _____

3. _____

4. _____

5. _____

Encore des verbes

1 These new words are all verbs. They belong to the **-RE** family. See if you can guess their meanings:

attendre

descendre

entendre

répondre

vendre

Here are 5 more action words (verbs). You have probably noticed, however, that they do not belong to the **-ER** or **-IR** family. To what family do these

verbs belong? _____ Just as we made changes in the **-ER** verbs by dropping the **-ER** and in the **-IR** verbs by dropping the **-IR** and adding certain endings, we must do the same thing with these verbs. The endings will be different. Let's see what happens. Read the story, look for the **-RE** verbs and see if you can spot the endings:

C'est samedi. Il est onze heures du soir. Michelle, Anne et Brigitte sont chez Brigitte. Les parents de Brigitte ne sont pas à la maison. Ils sont au théâtre. Les trois jeunes filles ont peur. Tout à coup Michelle dit:

MICHELLE: **Entendez-vous** quelque chose?
ANNE ET BRIGITTE: Non, **nous n'entendons rien.** Et toi? **Tu entends** quelque chose?

samedi *Saturday* **onze heures du soir** *11 P.M.*

ont peur *are afraid* **tout à coup** *suddenly*

quelque chose *something*
ne ... rien *nothing*

MICHELLE: Oui, **j'entends** quelque chose. Il y a quelqu'un dans la maison, Brigitte. J'ai peur.

quelqu'un *somebody*

Les trois jeunes filles descendent l'escalier. **Elles entendent** quelque chose. Tout à coup Brigitte rit. **Elle entend** un bruit.

l'escalier *the stairs*
rit *laughs*
un bruit *a noise*

BRIGITTE: Tu es folle, Michelle. Voilà! **Tu entends** mon chat? Il joue avec mon chien.

folle *crazy*

Activité

A. Oui ou Non? If the sentence is incorrect, change it to make it correct:

1. C'est dimanche (*Sunday*).

   _____

2. Il est huit heures du matin (*8 A.M.*).

   _____

3. Il y a trois garçons à la maison.

   _____

4. Elles sont chez Anne.

   _____

5. Elles ont faim.

   _____

6. Les filles entendent le professeur.

   _____

7. Elles descendent d'un autobus.

   _____

8. Les filles entendent deux animaux.

   _____

2 Now see if you can complete the correct endings by looking at the story. To

form the present tense of **-RE** verbs: Take the infinitive, drop _____, and
add these endings:

j'entend_____   nous entend_____

tu entend_____   vous entend_____

il entend_____   ils entend_____

elle entend_____   elles entend_____

NOTE: **J'entends.** What happens to the e in **je?** _____

What do we put in place of the e in **je?** _____

Why did we do this? _____

Activités

B. Let's practice with the other **-re** verbs:

	attendre	descendre	répondre	vendre
je	_____	_____	_____	_____
tu	_____	_____	_____	_____
il	_____	_____	_____	_____
elle	_____	_____	_____	_____
nous	_____	_____	_____	_____
vous	_____	_____	_____	_____
ils	_____	_____	_____	_____
elles	_____	_____	_____	_____

C. Fill in the correct subject pronoun:

1. _____ descends

2. _____ vendons

3. _____ entendent

4. _____ attends

5. _____ descendent

6. _____ attendez

7. _____ entend

8. _____ répond

D. Fill in the correct forms of the verbs. Be sure to drop all the **-re** endings before starting:

1. (attendre) Je _____ les parents.

2. (descendre) Nous _____ avec les touristes.

3. (entendre) Tu _____ une histoire intéressante.

4. (répondre) Vous _____ ici.

5. (vendre) Il _____ l'auto.

6. (attendre) Elles _____ les amies.

7. (descendre) Marie _____ de l'autobus.

8. (entendre) Paul et Alain _____ quelque chose.

9. (répondre) Sylvie et Régine _____ rapidement.

10. (vendre) Ils _____ les tickets.

E. Now make complete French sentences by putting in the correct verb form and an ending to the sentence:

1. (wait for) Je _____.

2. (descent) Elle _____.

3. (hear) Vous _____.

4. (answer) Paul et Anne _____.

5. (sell) Tu _____.

6. (wait for) Ils _____.

7. (descend) Nous _____.

128

8. (hears) Jeanne _____ .

9. (answers) Il _____ .

10. (sells) Elle _____ .

F. Match the sentences with the pictures they describe:

Tu vends la guitare.　　Vous descendez.
J'attends.　　　　　　Elle répond.
Il entend le professeur.

1. _____　　2. _____

3. _____　　4. _____

5. _____

G. Here are some **-re** verbs. See if you can match them with the English meanings. Write the matching number and letter in the space provided:

1. tu attends   **a.** I sell   _____

2. je vends   **b.** he descends _____

3. il descend   **c.** they answer _____

4. nous attendons   **d.** you hear   _____

5. vous entendez   **e.** she sells   _____

6. elles répondent   **f.** you wait for _____

7. ils entendent   **g.** they hear   _____

8. elle vend   **h.** we wait for _____

QUESTIONS PERSONNELLES

1. Entendez-vous le professeur? _____

2. Répondez-vous aux questions? _____

3. Attendez-vous des amis? _____

VOUS

Complete these 5 sentences by writing something original about yourself.

EXAMPLE: **J'attends**   **J'attends le garçon.**

1. J'attends _____

2. Je descends _____

3. J'entends _____

4. J'apprends _____

5. Je vends _____

CONVERSATION

Salut, Thérèse. Où est le chat, Tigre?

Tigre est à la maison. Il mange maintenant.

Tigre est un joli chat. Est-il intelligent?

Bien sûr. Quand il observe quelque chose, il apprend vite.

J'aimerais bien avoir un animal comme Tigre.

Veux-tu acheter Tigre?

Quel est le prix?

Un million de dollars.

VOCABULAIRE

joli *pretty*
il apprend *he learns*
j'aimerais bien *I'd love to*

acheter *to buy*
Quel est le prix? *How much is it?*

DIALOGUE

What would the second person in this dialog say? Circle your selections from the choices provided:

Salut, Marie. Où est le chien, Féroce?

> Féroce est au cinéma.
> Féroce est à la maison.
> Féroce est à l'école.

Féroce est un joli chien. Est-il intelligent?

> Oui, il entend vite.
> Oui, il descend vite.
> Oui, il apprend vite.

J'aimerais bien avoir un animal comme Féroce.

> Veux-tu acheter Féroce?
> Veux-tu vendre Féroce?
> Veux-tu entendre Féroce?

Quel est le prix?

> Un livre.
> Un million de dollars.
> La classe.

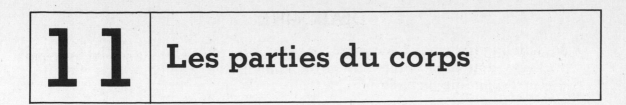

11 | Les parties du corps

1 LE MONSTRE

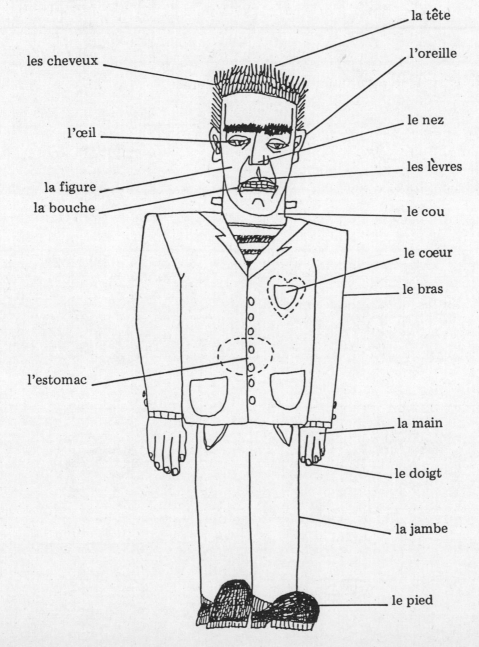

la tête
l'oreille
les cheveux
le nez
l'œil
les lèvres
la figure
la bouche
le cou
le cœur
le bras
l'estomac
la main
le doigt
la jambe
le pied

Activités

A. This monster may look weird, but the parts of his body are the same as yours and mine. Study them and match the French words with the corresponding pictures:

la figure	l'oreille	la langue
les cheveux	la bouche	les dents
les yeux (l'œil)	les lèvres	la tête
le nez		

1. _____

2. _____

3. _____

4. _____

5. _____

6. _____

7. _____

8. _____

9. _____

10. _____

134

B. Label these parts of the face:

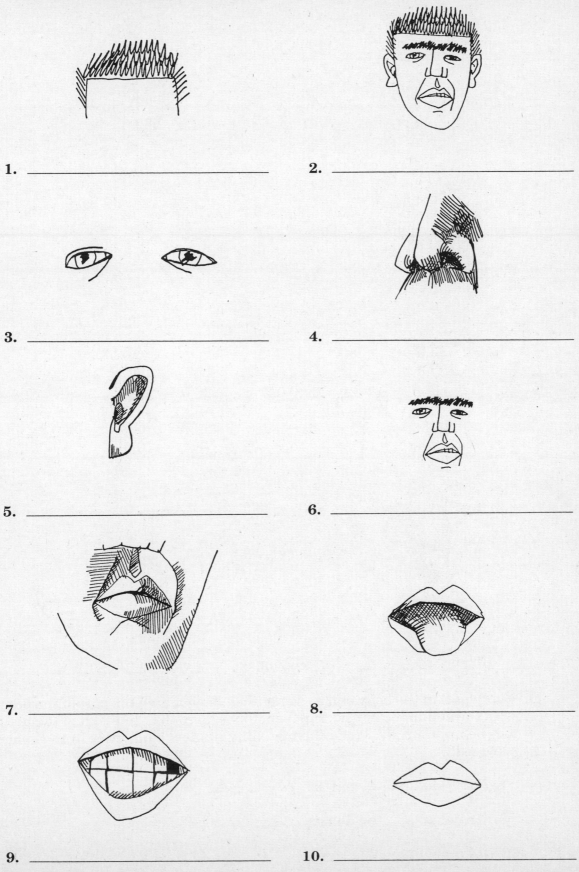

1. _____

2. _____

3. _____

4. _____

5. _____

6. _____

7. _____

8. _____

9. _____

10. _____

C. Now label some other parts of the body:

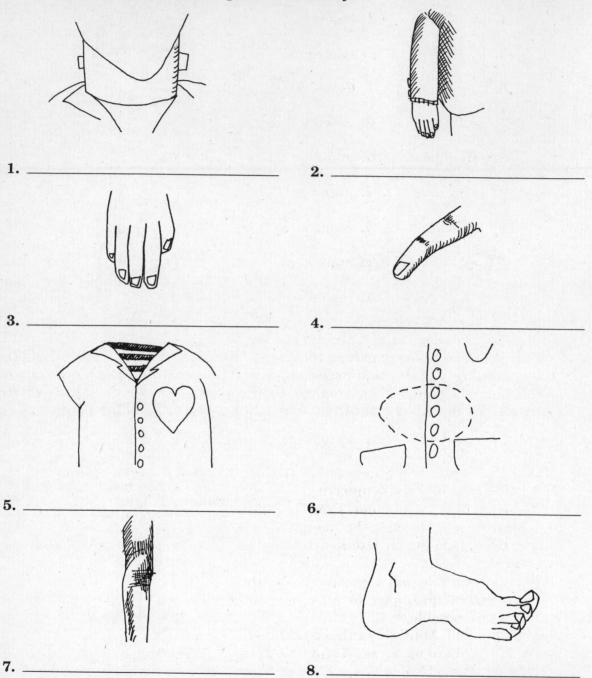

1. _____ 2. _____

3. _____ 4. _____

5. _____ 6. _____

7. _____ 8. _____

D. Every part of the body can do something. Now match the part of the body with the action it can perform. Sometimes more than one part of the body will be appropriate. Write the matching number and letter in the space provided:

    1. les pieds   **a.** parler   _____

    2. les dents   **b.** danser   _____

    3. les mains   **c.** chanter   _____

136

4. la bouche   **d.** étudier   _____

5. les lèvres   **e.** regarder   _____

6. les oreilles   **f.** descendre   _____

7. la langue   **g.** entendre   _____

8. la jambe   **h.** goûter   _____

9. le bras   **i.** marcher   _____

10. les yeux   **j.** écouter   _____

     k. applaudir

     l. répondre

2 Now that you are an expert on the parts of the body, you are ready to read the amazing story of the mad French scientist, Dr. François Frankenpierre, and the horrible monster he created. In this story are all the forms of the irregular French verb **avoir** (*to have*). See if you can find them all:

La création d'un MONSTRE

LIEU: Laboratoire d'un savant fou, le docteur François Frankenpierre.

lieu *place*   **un savant** *a scientist*   **fou** *crazy*

PERSONNAGES: Le docteur Frankenpierre; Marcel, son associé; Le monstre, une combinaison de différentes parties du corps.

son associé *his associate*

une combinaison *a combination*   **parties** *parts*

LE DOCTEUR FRANKENPIERRE parle: **J'ai** une idée magnifique. Je veux créer une créature terrible.

créer *to create*

MARCEL: Oui, Maître Frankenpierre.

maître *master*

DR. F.: D'abord un corps. **Avons-nous** un corps, Marcel?

d'abord *first*   **un corps** *a body*

MARCEL: **Vous avez** un corps ici, monsieur, un vieux corps laid.

vieux *old*   **laid** *ugly*

DR. F.: Bon. Bon. Et maintenant, deux bras, Marcel.

MARCEL: Voilà deux bras. **Ils ont** beaucoup de poils.

poils *(body) hair*

DR. F.: Bon. Et les mains?

MARCEL: Deux mains. Une main d'homme et l'autre de gorille.

l'autre *the other*

DR. F.: **Les mains ont** combien de doigts?

combien de *how many*

MARCEL: Dix doigts, monsieur.

DR. F.: Parfait.

MARCEL: Il y a sept doigts à une main et trois à l'autre.

DR. F.: Bon. Les pieds. **Avons-nous** des pieds?

MARCEL: Certainement, monsieur. Un grand pied et un autre qui est très petit.

DR. F.: Très bien. Mais **il n'a pas** de tête.

MARCEL: La voici, monsieur. Une petite tête avec une figure stupide.

DR. F.: Formidable. Un courant d'électricité va donner la vie au monstre. BZZZZZZZZZZZZ

MARCEL: Regardez le monstre. . . . Il désire parler!

DR. F.: **Tu as** la vie. Parle! Parle!

LE MONSTRE: Je parle, tu parles, il parle . . .

DR. F.: Quel monstre formidable! C'est un professeur de français. C'est (*Fill in the name of your French teacher*)

parfait *perfect*

certainement *certainly*

un courant *a current*
va *is going to*   **la vie** *life*

_____.

Activités

E. Oui ou Non? If the sentence is incorrect, change it to make it correct:

1. Le Docteur Frankenpierre est fou.

_____

2. Le monstre a le corps d'un jeune homme.

_____

3. Le monstre n'a pas de bras.

_____

4. Chaque main a 5 doigts.

_____

5. Le monstre danse bien.

_____

6. Le monstre a une figure intelligente.

_____

7. Le docteur emploie un courant d'électricité pour donner la vie au monstre.

_____

8. Le monstre parle italien.

_____

F. Fill in the names of the labeled parts of the body:

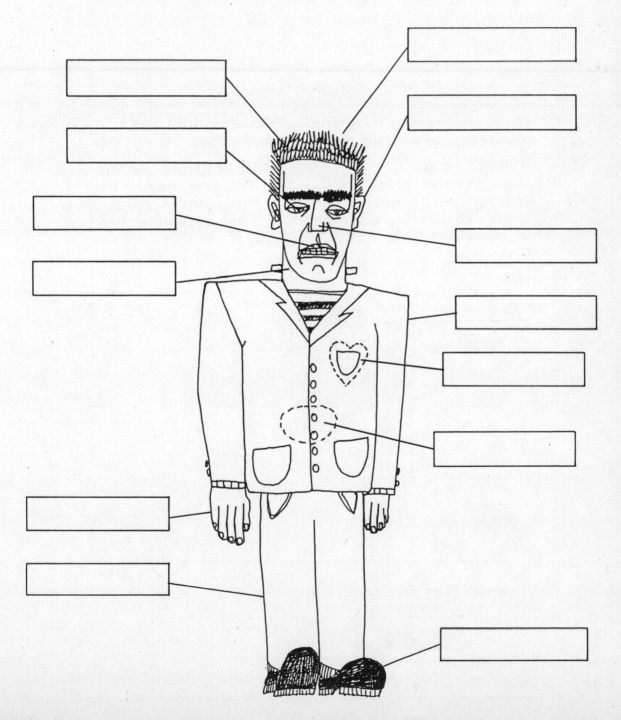

3 Can you find the forms of the irregular verb **avoir** in the story? Remember: **Avoir** is a special verb because it is one of a kind. No other verb in French is conjugated like **avoir. Avoir** means *to have.* Fill in the proper verb forms for each subject. MEMORIZE them:

j' _____   nous _____

tu _____   vous _____

il _____   ils _____

elle _____   elles _____

Activités

G. Here are some sentences in which a form of **avoir** is used. Can you match these sentences with the pictures they describe?

J'ai deux têtes.
Il a un grand cœur.
Nous avons dix doigts.
Elles ont les cheveux longs.
Vous avez de longues jambes.

Tu as deux bras forts.
Elle a un long cou.
Elle a des lèvres rouges.
Vous avez un grand nez.
Il n'a pas de cheveux.

1. _____

2. _____

3. _____

4. _____

5. _____

6. _____

7. _____

8. _____

9. _____

10. _____

H. Fill in the correct subject pronoun:

1. _____ avons les yeux verts.

2. _____ ont les cheveux longs.

3. _____ ai un petit nez.

4. _____ as de grandes oreilles.

5. _____ avez une grande tête.

6. _____ a dix doigts.

I. Fill in the correct form of the verb **avoir:**

   1. Tu _____ une petite tête.

   2. Il _____ un grand nez.

   3. Elles _____ deux jambes.

   4. Vous _____ deux pieds.

   5. J' _____ une bouche mince.

   6. Ils _____ deux oreilles.

   7. Elle _____ dix doigts.

   8. Pierre _____ deux mains.

   9. Les filles _____ les yeux bruns.

 10. Les garçons _____ les cheveux blonds.

 11. Marie _____ deux lèvres rouges.

 12. Elles _____ de jolis yeux.

J. Make all the sentences in Exercise I negative:

   1. _____

   2. _____

   3. _____

   4. _____

   5. _____

   6. _____

   7. _____

   8. _____

9. _____

10. _____

11. _____

12. _____

K. Change all the sentences in Exercise I to questions using inversion. Be careful if the subject is **je** or is NOT a pronoun:

1. _____

2. _____

3. _____

4. _____

5. _____

6. _____

7. _____

8. _____

9. _____

10. _____

11. _____

12. _____

4 More on **avoir**

There are a few very common expressions in French that use the verb **avoir**, while the comparable English expressions use the verb "to be":

avoir chaud	*to be warm*
avoir froid	*to be cold*
avoir faim	*to be hungry*
avoir soif	*to be thirsty*
avoir _____ ans	*to be _____ old*
avoir raison	*to be right*
avoir tort	*to be wrong*
avoir sommeil	*to be sleepy*

EXAMPLES: **J'ai faim.** *I am hungry.*
Il a soif. *He is thirsty.*

143

Activités

L. Match the French expressions with the English meanings. Write the number and matching letter in the space provided:

1. Nous avons faim.   **a.** She is thirsty.   _____

2. Elle a soif.   **b.** He is hot.   _____

3. J'ai froid.   **c.** You are sleepy.   _____

4. Il a chaud.   **d.** Paul is 15 years old.   _____

5. Paul a quinze ans.   **e.** They are right.   _____

6. Tu as sommeil.   **f.** Are you hungry?   _____

7. Ils ont raison.   **g.** How old are you?   _____

8. Vous avez tort.   **h.** We are hungry.   _____

9. Quel âge avez-vous?   **i.** I'm cold.   _____

10. As-tu faim?   **j.** You're wrong.   _____

M. Choose the English expression that is equivalent to the French expression:

1. Vous avez très soif. _____
   (a) You're very hungry.   (b) You're very thirsty.   (c) We're very tired.   (d) He's right.

2. Tu n'as pas raison. _____
   (a) He is not wrong.   (b) You are not cold.   (c) You are not right.   (d) They aren't sleepy.

3. A-t-il sommeil? _____
   (a) Is she hungry?   (b) Are they thirsty?   (c) Are you cold?   (d) Is he sleepy?

4. N'a-t-elle pas froid? _____
   (a) Is she cold?   (b) She's not cold.   (c) Isn't she cold?   (d) Isn't she hot?

5. Il a vingt ans. _____
   (a) He's 20 years old.   (b) He has 20 friends.   (c) He has $20.   (d) Is he 20 years old?

144

N. Label the pictures:

L'enfant a un an.   **Elle a chaud.**
Les hommes ont faim.   **Il a froid.**
J'ai soif.   **Le bébé a sommeil.**

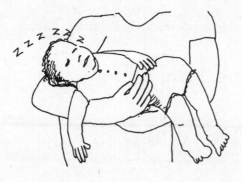

1. _____

2. _____

3. _____

4. _____

5. _____

6. _____

O. Write in French:

1. I'm hungry. _____

2. He's sleepy. _____

3. You're cold. _____

4. We are right. _____

5. They are wrong. _____

QUESTIONS PERSONNELLES

1. Quel âge avez-vous?

_____

2. Combien de dents avez-vous?

_____

3. Avez-vous faim?

_____

4. Comment allez-vous?

_____

5. Avez-vous sommeil?

_____

VOUS

Draw yourself as you would like to look and label the parts of your body.

CONVERSATION

Salut, Caroline. Comment vas-tu?

Je ne vais pas bien, docteur. Je suis malade.

Pauvre jeune fille. Qu'est-ce que tu as?

Je ne veux pas manger. Je ne veux pas regarder la télé. Je souffre beaucoup.

Tu as la grippe, Caroline.

Est-ce que je dois aller à l'hôpital?

Pas du tout. Mais tu dois prendre des médicaments. Reste deux ou trois jours à la maison.

Oh, merci, docteur.

VOCABULAIRE

Comment vas-tu? *How are you?*
Je ne vais pas bien *I'm not well*
Je suis malade *I'm sick*
pauvre *poor*
Qu'est-ce que tu as? *What's the matter with you?*

la grippe *the flu*
aller *to go*
pas du tout *not at all*
prendre *to take*
le médicament *the medication, medicine*
rester *to stay, to remain*

DIALOGUE

Fill in the words that are missing in the dialog. Choose from the list provided below:

Salut, Caroline. Comment _____-tu?

    Je ne _____ pas bien, docteur, Je suis _____

    _____.

Pauvre jeune fille. Qu'est-ce que tu _____?

    Je ne veux pas _____. Je ne veux pas _____

    _____. Je _____ beaucoup.

Tu as _____, Caroline.

    Est-ce que je dois aller à _____?

Pas du tout. Mais tu dois prendre des _____. Reste à la

_____ pendant 2 ou 3 _____.

    Oh _____, docteur.

médicaments	vais	merci
manger	souffre	as
fille	jours	malade
travailler	la grippe	l'hôpital
maison	vas	

148

1985

	JANVIER	FÉVRIER	MARS	AVRIL
LUNDI	7 14 21 28	4 11 18 25	4 11 18 25	1 8 15 22 29
MARDI	1 8 15 22 29	5 12 19 26	5 12 19 26	2 9 16 23 30
MERCREDI	2 9 16 23 30	6 13 20 27	6 13 20 27	3 10 17 24
JEUDI	3 10 17 24 31	7 14 21 28	7 14 21 28	4 11 18 25
VENDREDI	4 11 18 25	1 8 15 22	1 8 15 22 29	5 12 19 26
SAMEDI	5 12 19 26	2 9 16 23	2 9 16 23 30	6 13 20 27
DIMANCHE	6 13 20 27	3 10 17 24	3 10 17 24 31	7 14 21 28

	MAI	JUIN	JUILLET	AOÛT
LUNDI	6 13 20 27	3 10 17 24	1 8 15 22 29	5 12 19 26
MARDI	7 14 21 28	4 11 18 25	2 9 16 23 30	6 13 20 27
MERCREDI	1 8 15 22 29	5 12 19 26	3 10 17 24 31	7 14 21 28
JEUDI	2 9 16 23 30	6 13 20 27	4 11 18 25	1 8 15 22 29
VENDREDI	3 10 17 24 31	7 14 21 28	5 12 19 26	2 9 16 23 30
SAMEDI	4 11 18 25	1 8 15 22 29	6 13 20 27	3 10 17 24 31
DIMANCHE	5 12 19 26	2 9 16 23 30	7 14 21 28	4 11 18 25

	SEPTEMBRE	OCTOBRE	NOVEMBRE	DÉCEMBRE
LUNDI	2 9 16 23 30	7 14 21 28	4 11 18 25	2 9 16 23 30
MARDI	3 10 17 24	1 8 15 22 29	5 12 19 26	3 10 17 24 31
MERCREDI	4 11 18 25	2 9 16 23 30	6 13 20 27	4 11 18 25
JEUDI	5 12 19 26	3 10 17 24 31	7 14 21 28	5 12 19 26
VENDREDI	6 13 20 27	4 11 18 25	1 8 15 22 29	6 13 20 27
SAMEDI	7 14 21 28	5 12 19 26	2 9 16 23 30	7 14 21 28
DIMANCHE	1 8 15 22 29	6 13 20 27	3 10 17 24	1 8 15 22 29

1 **Les jours de la semaine sont:**

lundi	mardi	mercredi	jeudi
vendredi	samedi	dimanche	

Activités

A. Fill in the name of the day of the week:

1. l＿n＿i   **2.** ve＿dr＿＿i   **3.** m＿＿d＿   **4.** ＿e＿＿i

5. m＿r＿＿＿d＿   **6.** s＿＿＿＿i   **7.** d＿m＿＿＿＿e

B. Fill in the correct information:

1. Il y a _____ jours dans une semaine.

2. Les jours de travail (*work*) sont _____

_____.

3. Il n'y a pas de classes le _____ et le _____.

C. Fill in the days before and after the day given:

1. _____ lundi _____

2. _____ mercredi _____

3. _____ vendredi _____

4. _____ dimanche _____

2 Now you can read this story about the days of the week:

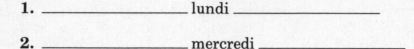

Quel est votre jour favori? Pourquoi?

RAOUL: Samedi et dimanche. Il n'y a pas de classes.

FRANÇOISE: Lundi. J'aime aller à l'école.

SYLVIE: Lundi, mardi, mercredi, jeudi et vendredi. Je parle avec Paul, un garçon formidable dans la classe d'histoire.

ROGER: Samedi et dimanche. J'aime regarder les sports à la télé.

HERVÉ: Samedi. J'ai rendez-vous tous les samedis avec une jeune fille différente.

ANNE: Mercredi. J'ai un cours de karaté. J'aime me défendre.

rendez-vous *a date*

un cours *a course*

Activités

D. Match the person with his/her favorite day. Write the number and matching letter in the space provided:

1. Anne **a.** samedi _____

2. Sylvie **b.** lundi _____

3. Raoul **c.** mercredi _____

4. Hervé **d.** samedi et dimanche _____

5. Françoise **e.** dimanche _____

6. Roger **f.** lundi, mardi, mercredi, jeudi, vendredi _____

E. Give the reason in French why each person prefers his/her favorite day:

1. Roger _____

2. Anne _____

3. Raoul _____

4. Françoise _____

5. Hervé _____

6. Sylvie _____

F. Quel est votre jour favori? _____

    Pourquoi? _____

3 Look at the spelling of the days of the week. What do you notice about the first

letters of each day when they appear in the middle of the sentence? _____

_____

How does each day end except for **dimanche?** _____

How does **dimanche** begin? _____

4 Les mois de l'année sont:

janvier

février

mars

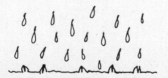

avril

mai

juin

151

juillet

août

septembre

octobre

novembre

décembre

G. Complete the names of the months:

1. j _ n _ _ _ r
2. m _ _ s
3. o _ t _ _ _ e
4. a _ _ t
5. n o _ e _ b _ _
6. j _ _ n
7. f _ _ r _ _ r
8. a _ _ _ l
9. m _ _
10. d _ _ e _ b _ _
11. j _ _ _ _ _ t
12. s e _ _ _ m b r e

H. Fill in the months before and after the month given:

_____ février _____

_____ mai _____

_____ août _____

_____ novembre _____

_____ janvier _____

_____ avril _____

_____ juillet _____

_____ octobre _____

5 **Les quatre saisons sont:**

le printemps   l'été   l'automne   l'hiver

I. Fill in the names of the months for each season:

le printemps   l'été   l'automne   l'hiver

m _____   j _____   s _____   d _____

a _____   j _____   o _____   j _____

m _____   a _____   n _____   f _____

6 Now you can read this story about the months of the year:

Quelle est votre saison favorite? Quel est votre mois favori? Pourquoi?

RÉGINE: L'hiver. Janvier. J'aime faire du ski.
MARIE: L'été. Août. J'aime nager dans l'océan.
ARTHUR: L'automne. Octobre. J'aime jouer au football américain.
ANDRÉ: Le printemps. Avril. J'aime jouer au baseball.
CHANTAL: L'automne. Septembre. J'aime la rentrée des classes.
PAUL: L'été. Juillet. J'aime les grandes vacances.
ÉRIC: L'hiver. Décembre. J'aime Noël.
MICHÈLE: Le printemps. Mai. J'aime les jolies fleurs.

Activités

J. Match the person with his/her favorite month. Write the number and matching letter in the space provided:

1. Paul   **a.** mai   _____

2. André   **b.** janvier   _____

3. Michèle   **c.** décembre   _____

4. Arthur   **d.** avril   _____

5. Régine   **e.** juillet   _____

6. Éric   **f.** octobre   _____

7. Marie   **g.** août   _____

8. Chantal   **h.** septembre   _____

K. Give the reason in French why each person prefers his/her month:

1. Éric _____

2. Michèle _____

3. Marie _____

4. André _____

5. Chantal _____

6. Paul _____

7. Régine _____

8. Arthur _____

L. Quelle est votre saison favorite? _____

Pourquoi? _____

Quel est votre mois favori? _____

Pourquoi? _____

M. Name the season for each month:

1. mars _____

2. juillet _____

3. octobre _____

4. janvier _____

5. décembre _____

6. mai _____

7. août _____

8. avril _____

9. novembre _____

10. juin _____

11. septembre _____

12. février _____

154

7 Look at the spelling of the months and the seasons. What do you notice about the first letters when these words are in the middle of the sentence?

_____

8 Now let's see how the French express the date:

Quelle est la date aujourd'hui? (*What is today's date?*)

```
  SEPTEMBRE
  3 10 17 24
  4 11 18 25
  5 12 19 26
  6 13 20 27
  7 14 21 28
1  8 15 22 29
(2) 9 16 23 30
```

C'est le deux septembre.

```
   JUILLET
2  9  16 23 30
3 10 17 24 31
4 (11) 18 25
5 12 19 26
6 13 20 27
7 14 21 28
8 15 22 29
```

C'est le onze juillet.

```
    MARS
 5  12 19 26
 6  13 (20) 27
 7  14 21 28
1 8  15 22 29
2 9  16 23 30
3 10 17 24 31
4 11 18 25
```

C'est le vingt mars.

```
    JANVIER
2  9  16 23 30
3 10 17 24 (31)
4 11 18 25
5 12 19 26
6 13 20 27
7 14 21 28
1  8 15 22 29
```

C'est le trente et un janvier.

Can you fill in the blanks? To express the date use:

C'est + _____ + _____ + _____

There is just one exception: **Quelle est la date aujourd'hui?**

```
    AOÛT
 6  13 20 27
 7  14 21 28
(1) 8  15 22 29
2 9  16 23 30
3 10 17 24 31
4 11 18 25
5 12 19 26
```

C'est le premier août.

To express the date when speaking about the *first* day of the month use:

C'est + _____ + _____ + _____

If you want to include the day of the week: **C'est lundi, le trois mai:**

C'est + _____, + _____ + _____

+ _____

Activités

N. Express these dates in French:

    1. April 22 _____

    2. August 7 _____

    3. February 1 _____

    4. July 29 _____

    5. January 12 _____

    6. Monday, March 30 _____

    7. Saturday, December 4 _____

    8. Wednesday, June 15 _____

    9. Sunday, September 14 _____

   10. Thursday, November 16 _____

   11. Tuesday, May 13 _____

   12. Friday, October 21 _____

O. Give the dates in French for these important events:

    1. your birthday _____

    2. Christmas _____

    3. New Year's Day _____

    4. Independence Day _____

    5. your favorite day of the year _____

P. Make a list of five dates that are important to you. Tell why in French. Choose from the list of reasons given:

EXAMPLES: **mon anniversaire** (*my birthday*) _____ le onze juillet _____

l'anniversaire de mon frère   _____
l'anniversaire de ma sœur
l'anniversaire de ma mère   _____
l'anniversaire de mon père
l'anniversaire de mariage de mes parents   _____
Noël
Pâques   _____
le Jour de l'An

    _____

9   Now you can read this story about dates:

Quelle est votre date favorite? Pourquoi?

RAOUL: Le vingt-cinq décembre. J'aime l'arbre de Noël et toutes les décorations.
    l'arbre *the tree*

FRANÇOISE: Le quatre juillet. J'aime voir le feu d'artifice.
    le feu d'artifice *the fireworks*

SYLVIE: Le quinze avril. C'est mon anniversaire. J'aime les cadeaux.
    les cadeaux *the gifts*

ROGER: Le premier janvier. Je mange un grand dîner dans un restaurant élégant.

HERVÉ: Le onze juillet. C'est mon anniversaire. Je mange du gâteau.
    le gâteau *the cake*

ANNE: Le premier juillet. L'école finit et les vacances commencent.
    les vacances *the vacation*

Activités

Q. Match the person with his/her favorite date. Write the number and matching letter in the space provided:

1. Anne   **a.** le vingt-cinq décembre _____

2. Sylvie   **b.** le quatre juillet _____

3. Raoul   **c.** le quinze avril _____

4. Hervé   **d.** le onze juillet _____

5. Françoise   **e.** le premier juillet _____

6. Roger   **f.** le premier janvier _____

R. Give the reason in French why each person prefers his/her favorite date:

1. Roger _____

2. Anne _____

3. Raoul _____

4. Françoise _____

5. Hervé _____

6. Sylvie _____

QUESTIONS PERSONNELLES

1. Quelle est la date d'aujourd'hui? _____

2. Quelle est la date de votre anniversaire? _____

3. Quelle est votre saison favorite? _____

4. En quelle saison avez-vous froid? _____

5. En quelle saison avez-vous chaud? _____

VOUS

1. Name your favorite day(s) of the week and tell why you prefer it (them):
   EXAMPLE: **J'aime le samedi. Je ne travaille pas.**

   _____

2. Name your favorite month(s) and tell why:
   EXAMPLE: **J'aime le mois de juillet. J'aime l'été.**

   _____

3. Name your favorite season and tell why:
   EXAMPLE: **J'aime l'été. J'aime aller à la plage.**

   _____

Révision III (Leçons 9-12)

Leçon 9

a. The verb **être** is an irregular verb that means *to be*. All of its forms must be memorized:

je *suis*	nous *sommes*
tu *es*	vous *êtes*
il *est*	ils *sont*
elle *est*	elles *sont*

b. The same rules as the rules for **-er** verbs apply for making a sentence negative or for asking a question.

Leçon 10

a. To conjugate verbs that belong to the **-RE** family, drop **-RE** from the infinitive:

EXAMPLE: **vendre**

If the subject is		add		to the remaining stem:	
	je	add	s		je vends
	tu		s		tu vends
	il		–		il vend
	elle		–		elle vend
	nous		ons		nous vendons
	vous		ez		vous vendez
	ils		ent		ils vendent
	elles		ent		elles vendent

b. The same rules as the rules for **-er** verbs apply for making a sentence negative or for asking a question, except that no **-t-** is needed for inversion with **il** or **elle**.

Leçon 11

a. The verb **avoir** is an irregular verb that means **to have**. All of its verb forms must be memorized:

j'*ai*	nous *avons*
tu *as*	vous *avez*
il *a*	ils *ont*
elle *a*	elles *ont*

b. Learn the meanings of these special expressions that use **avoir**. They may be used with any subject as long as **avoir** is conjugated:

avoir chaud	*to be hot, warm*	**avoir _____ ans**	*to be _____ years old*
avoir faim	*to be hungry*	**avoir raison**	*to be right*
avoir froid	*to be cold*	**avoir tort**	*to be wrong*
avoir soif	*to be thirsty*	**avoir sommeil**	*to be sleepy*

EXAMPLES: **J'ai chaud.**   *I'm warm.*
Nous avons faim.   *We are hungry.*

c. The same rules as the rules for **-er** verbs apply for making a sentence negative or for asking a question. When there is inversion with **il** or **elle**, **-t-** must be put between the verb and the subject. (Do not invert with **je**.):

as-tu?   **est-ce que j'ai?**
a-t-il?
a-t-elle?
avons-nous?
avez-vous?
ont-ils?
ont-elles?

Leçon 12

LES JOURS	LES MOIS	LES SAISONS
lundi	janvier	l'hiver
mardi	février	
mercredi	mars	
jeudi	avril	le printemps
vendredi	mai	
samedi	juin	
dimanche	juillet	l'été
	août	
	septembre	
	octobre	l'automne
	novembre	
	décembre	

Activités

A. Write the French word next to the English word. Then find the French word in the puzzle:

postman _____   hair _____

fireman _____   eyes _____

lawyer _____   mouth_____

160

nurse	_____	head	_____
doctor	_____	nose	_____
secretary	_____	hand	_____
teacher	_____	foot	_____
dentist	_____	neck	_____
face	_____	arm	_____

```
U  E  S  F  I  G  U  R  E  E  T
C  O  R  A  X  U  E  V  E  H  C
T  S  C  C  R  P  Y  G  T  R  R
D  E  N  T  I  S  T  E  U  E  P
O  C  A  E  F  U  T  E  U  V  R
C  R  D  U  I  E  S  O  A  X  E
T  E  M  R  B  S  X  V  C  H  I
E  T  R  A  E  R  O  U  C  I  P
U  A  E  F  I  C  A  U  N  A  M
R  I  O  D  A  N  O  S  T  Z  O
E  R  N  T  I  B  C  U  E  E  P
P  E  R  E  I  M  R  I  F  N  I
```

B. Jumble: Unscramble the words. Then unscramble the letters in the circles to find out the message:

EUJID ⊡□⊡□□

CHIMADNE □⊡□□□□□□

ETRATNDE □□⊡□□□□⊡

MLESMOI ⊡⊡□□⊡□⊡

Jean dit à son amie Sylvie: _____

161

C. Place the words describing the pictures in their proper places:

3 lettres

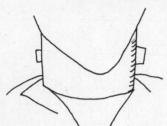   

4 lettres

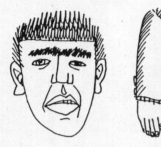

5 lettres

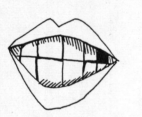 

6 lettres

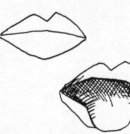  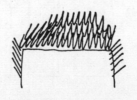 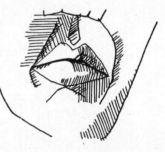

7 lettres

 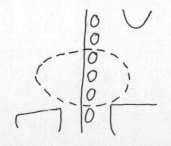

162

163

D. Acrostique: After filling in all the horizontal boxes, look at the vertical box. You will find a mystery word:

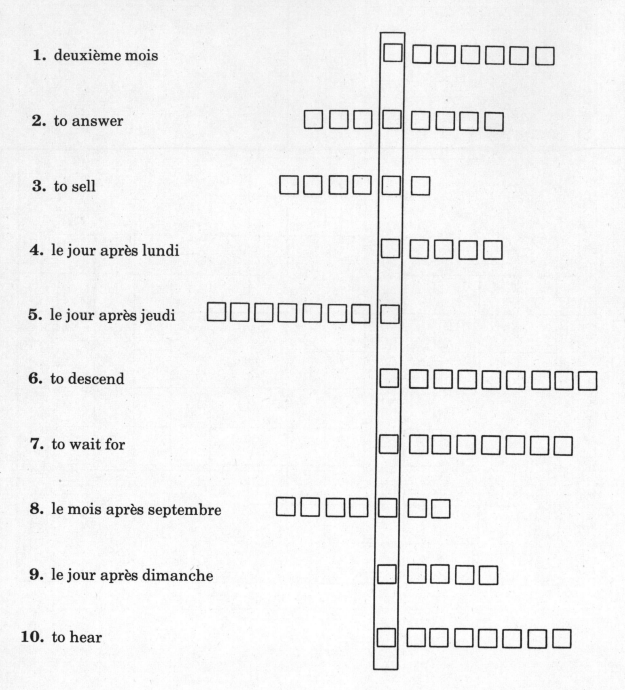

1. deuxième mois

2. to answer

3. to sell

4. le jour après lundi

5. le jour après jeudi

6. to descend

7. to wait for

8. le mois après septembre

9. le jour après dimanche

10. to hear

164

E. Each person has a problem. What is it?

1. _____

2. _____

3. _____

4. _____

5. _____

F. Picture Story

Can you read this story? Much of it is in picture form. Whenever you come to a picture, read it as if it were a French word:

Bonjour. Je m'appelle Robert. J'ai 12 ans. Je suis un intelligent.

J'ai les bleus et les blonds. Je suis sérieux à l'

Papa est . Maman est . Je veux être .

J'aime les aventures et j'ai les et les très

.

Bonjour. Je m'appelle Sylvie. J'ai 13 ans. Je suis une intelligente.

J'ai la jolie. J' toujours les professeurs. Papa

est et maman est . J'aime les 4 saisons: ,

, et . Je veux être . J'aime

beaucoup et apporter des aux gens.

166

Achievement Test I (Lessons 1–12)

1 Vocabulary [15 points]

A. Label the following items in French:

1. _____

2. _____

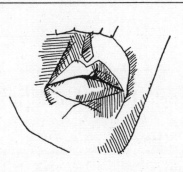

3. _____

4. _____

5. _____

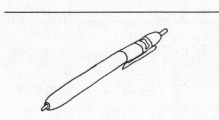

6. _____

7. _____

8. _____

9. _____ 10. _____

B. **Vrai ou Faux?** Tell whether the following statements are true of false. If they are false, correct them:

1. Le professeur travaille dans l'hôpital. _____

2. Le tigre est un animal timide. _____

3. Une semaine a sept mois. _____

4. Trois et douze font seize. _____

5. Je mange avec le nez. _____

2 Definite articles (**le, la, les**) and indefinite articles (**un, une, des**) [10 points]

1. (the) _____ sœur   2. (the) _____ dents

3. (the) _____ cheveux   4. (the) _____ tête

5. (the) _____ dictionnaire 6. (a) _____ craie

7. (an) _____ oreille   8. (some) _____ parents

9. (a) _____ bureau   10. (some) _____ photos

3 Action words (**-er, -ir, -re** verbs) [20 points]

1. chanter   Nous (*sing*) _____ en classe.

2. punir   Le père (*punishes*) _____ l'enfant.

3. attendre   J' (*wait for*) _____ la réponse.

4. applaudir   Vous (*applaud*) _____ au théâtre.

5. préparer   Tu (*prepare*) _____ le dîner.

6. descendre   Ils (*get off*) _____ de l'autobus.

7. jouer   Elles (*play*) _____ au football.

168

8. finir   Je (*finish*) _____ les devoirs.

9. demander   Paul (*asks for*) _____ le livre.

10. entendre   Nous (*hear*) _____ le programme.

11. remplir   Nous (*fill*) _____ les verres.

12. trouver   Je (*find*) _____ le dictionnaire.

13. travailler   Elle (*works*) _____ beaucoup.

14. répondre   Vous (*answer*) _____ correctement.

15. choisir   Tu (*choose*) _____ les crayons.

16. parler   Vous (*speak*) _____ bien.

17. chercher   Marie (*looks for*) _____ le restaurant.

18. vendre   Il (*sells*) _____ la maison.

19. saisir   Elles (*seize*) _____ le petit chat.

20. donner   Ils (*give*) _____ les stylos au professeur.

4 Negative and interrogative sentences [10 points]

A. Make the following sentences negative:

1. Elles mangent le dîner.

   _____

2. Alice finit le livre.

   _____

3. Les élèves répondent aux questions.

   _____

4. Nous choisissons un programme intéressant.

   _____

5. Vous écoutez en classe.

   _____

B. Make the following sentences into questions by using inversion:

1. Tu parles français.

   _____

2. Nous applaudissons après le programme.

   _____

3. Il arrive à l'école.

   _____

4. Marie chante bien.

   _____

5. Les docteurs attendent les victimes.

   _____

5 Fill in the correct form of the verb **être** [5 points]

1. Le chien _____ formidable.

2. Qui _____-vous?

3. Je _____ le professeur.

4. Nous _____ intelligents.

5. _____-ils américains?

6 Fill in the correct form of the verb **avoir** [5 points]

1. J'_____ quinze ans.

2. _____-nous raison?

3. _____-tu faim?

4. Vous _____ chaud.

5. Elle _____ sommeil.

7 Numbers [10 points]

Write out the number:

1. Deux et deux font _____.

2. Quatre et deux font _____.

3. Six et deux font _____.

4. Trois fois cinq font _____.

5. Dix moins cinq font _____.

6. Dix divisé par cinq font _____.

7. Quatre fois quatre font _____.

8. Neuf moins sept font _____.

9. Quinze et cinq font _____.

10. Dix-huit divisé par deux font _____.

8 Adjectives [10 points]

1. (the *strong* man)   l'homme _____

2. (the *French* girl)   la fille _____

3. (the *cruel* tigers)   les tigres _____

4. (the *red* book)   le livre _____

5. (the *elegant* woman)   le femme _____

6. (the *ugly* dogs)   les chiens _____

7. (the *comfortable* house) la maison _____

8. (the *different* rulers) les règles _____

9. (the *big* monsters)   les _____ monstres

10. (the *young* teacher)   le _____ professeur

9 Days and Months [10 points]

1. C'est aujourd'hui mardi. Demain est _____ .

2. Les jours du week-end sont le _____ et le dimanche.

3. Le premier jour de travail est _____ .

4. Il y a _____ jours dans une semaine.

5. Le premier mois est _____ .

6. Le dernier (*last*) mois est _____ .

7. Il y a trente jours aux mois de septembre, avril, juin et _____ .

8. Il y a trente et un jours aux mois de janvier, mai, juillet, août, décembre et

   _____ .

9. Il y a vingt-huit ou vingt-neuf jours au mois de _____ .

10. Il n'y a pas de classes aux mois de _____ et _____

    _____ .

10 Expressions [5 points]

Answer the following questions:

1. Comment vous appelez-vous?

   _____

2. Comment allez-vous?

   _____

3. Quel âge avez-vous?

   _____

4. Où est-ce que le professeur travaille?

   _____

5. Combien de dents avez-vous?

   _____

172

Quatrième Partie

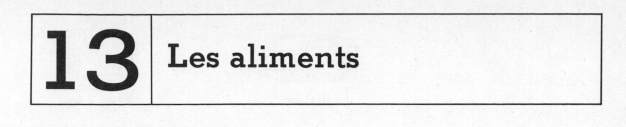

13 | Les aliments

1 You should like learning this new vocabulary:

la viande

la soupe

la salade

la tomate

la laitue

la glace

l'eau

l'orangeade

l'argent

le café

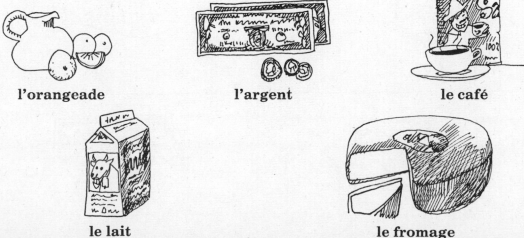

le lait

le fromage

le pain

le thon

le jambon

le poisson

les sandwiches (*m*)

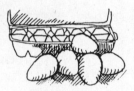

les pommes (*f*)

**les pommmes
de terre** (*f*)

les fruits (*m*)

les oeufs (*m*)

les légumes (*m*)

Activités

A. Identifiez:

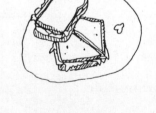

1. _____   2. _____

3. _____   4. _____

5. _____

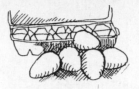

6. _____

7. _____

8. _____

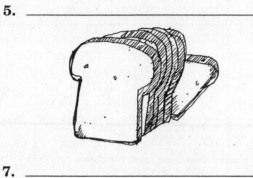

9. _____

10. _____

11. _____

12. _____

B. Fill in the correct definite article **le, la, l', les:**

1. _____pommes   2. _____orangeade

3. _____laitue   4. _____soupe

5. _____argent   6. _____œufs

7. _____eau   8. _____fromage

9. _____jambon   10. _____salade

11. _____pain   12. _____lait

177

C. Fill in the names of the foods shown in the drawings:

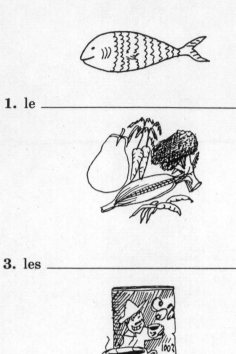

1. le _____

2. la _____

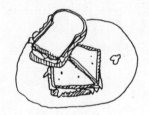

3. les _____

4. l' _____

5. le _____

6. la _____

7. les _____

8. l' _____

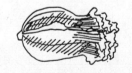

9. la _____

10. la _____

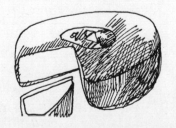

11. les _____

12. le _____

178

2 Now see if you can read this story and answer questions about it. All of the phrases in bold type begin with **du, de la, de l'**, or **des.** In this story, all of these words mean *some*:

La classe de français fait un pique-nique. Les élèves de la classe préparent **des spécialités françaises.** Ils apportent les spécialités au pique-nique.

fait *makes*

apportent *bring*

Alain apporte **de la bouillabaisse.** La bouillabaisse est une soupe préparée avec **du poisson.** C'est la spécialité de Marseille.

Suzette apporte une quiche. La quiche est préparée avec **du jambon, du fromage, du lait, des œufs** et **des épices.** La quiche est le plat typique de la Lorraine.

des épices *spices*
le plat *the dish*

Marie apporte **des œufs durs** et **des sandwiches** préparés avec **de la viande, des tomates** et **de la laitue.** Elle apporte aussi une salade niçoise. La salade niçoise est préparée avec **du thon, des radis** et **des légumes.** C'est la spécialité de Nice, une ville dans le Midi.

des radis *radishes*
une ville *a city*
le Midi *the South*

Hervé apporte le dessert. C'est **de la mousse au chocolat.** Tous les élèves adorent la mousse parce qu'elle est préparée avec **du chocolat, de la crème, des œufs et du cognac.** C'est la spécialité du professeur de la classe de français.

la crème *the cream*

Activités

D. Finissez les phrases:

1. Les élèves préparent _____ françaises.

2. La bouillabaisse est _____ préparée avec _____.

3. La bouillabaisse est la spécialité de _____.

4. La quiche est préparée avec _____ _____.

5. La quiche est la spécialité de _____.

6. Marie prépare une salade niçoise avec _____ _____.

7. Une salade niçoise est la spécialité de _____.

8. Le professeur prépare la mousse avec _____

_____.

E. Répondez aux questions:

1. Que fait la classe?

_____

2. Qu'est-ce qu'Alain apporte au pique-nique?

_____

3. Quel est le plat typique de la Lorraine?

_____

4. Qui apporte la quiche?

_____

5. Qu'est-ce que Marie apporte au pique-nique?

_____

6. Comment Marie prépare-t-elle les sandwiches?

_____

7. Qu'est-ce que c'est que Nice?

_____

8. Qui apporte le dessert?

_____

9. Quel dessert apporte-t-il?

_____

10. Pourquoi les élèves aiment-ils beaucoup la mousse?

_____

3 Now let's see if you can figure out how to use the partitive. Look carefully at the following groups of phrases:

I	II	III	IV
de la viande	*de l'*eau	*du* café	*des* sandwiches
de la salade	*de l'*orangeade	*du* lait	*des* pommes
de la soupe	*de l'*argent	*du* fromage	*des* fruits

In Group I, what is the gender of all of the nouns? _____

How do you know? _____

What little word did we put before **la?** _____

What does **de la** mean here? _____

In Group II, what is the gender of all of the nouns? _____

How do you know? _____

If the gender is not important in Group II, then something else must be important. Look at all of the nouns in Group II. They all have something in common. Look carefully at their beginnings. How are the nouns similar?

_____

What little word did we put before **l'?** _____

What does **de l'** mean here? _____

In Group III what is the gender of all of the nouns? _____

How do you know? _____

What little word did we use before all of the nouns? _____

What two little words did we combine to get **du?** _____

What does **du** mean? _____   _____

In Group IV what is the gender of all the nouns? _____

How do you know? _____

If the gender is not important in Group IV then something else must be important. Look at all of the nouns in Group IV. They all have something in common. Look carefully at their endings. How are the nouns similar?

_____

What little word did we put before all of the nouns? _____

What two little words did we combine to get **des**? _____

What does **des** mean? _____

de la, du, de l', and **des** express the partitive. Why do you think they are called "partitive"? _____

Activités

F. Fill in the correct form of the partitive:

1. _____ viande   2. _____ sandwiches

3. _____ orangeade   4. _____ café

5. _____ salade   6. _____ argent

7. _____ fruits   8. _____ fromage

9. _____ pain   10. _____ pommes

11. _____ poisson   12. _____ lait

13. _____ eau   14. _____ œufs

15. _____ laitue

G. Fill in any correct noun:

1. du _____   2. de la _____

3. des _____   4. de l' _____

5. du _____   6. de la _____

7. des _____   8. de l' _____

9. du _____   10. de la _____

11. des _____   12. de l' _____

H. Qu'est-ce que vous apportez à un pique-nique?

J'apporte

1. _____

2. _____

3. _____

4. _____

5. _____

6. _____

7. _____

8. _____

9. _____

10. _____

4 Now look carefully at the following sentences:

> Je **n'**apporte **pas** de sandwiches.
> Elle **n'**a **pas** de salade.
> Vous **ne** mangez **pas** de jambon.
> Nous **ne** préparons **pas** d'orangeade.

What do the words in bold type tell you about each sentence?

Underline the word in each sentence that stands for "any" or "some." What happens to the partitive article (**du, de la, de l', des**) in a negative sentence?

_____

What happens to **de** before a vowel? _____

Activité

I. Make the sentences negative. Remember to change the partitive article:

EXAMPLE: Elle prépare **des** sandwiches.
Elle **ne** prépare **pas de** sandwiches.

1. Tu as de l'eau. _____

2. Ils apportent des légumes. _____

183

3. Je mange de la viande. _____

4. Vous préparez du jambon. _____

5. Elle demande de la glace. _____

CHARLES LE CUISINIER

Charles the cook has prepared the three meals for today. Can you tell in French what they consist of? Choose from the list of foods on the right.

Le petit déjeuner

_____

_____

_____

_____

Le déjeuner

_____

_____

_____

Le dîner

_____

_____

_____

le poisson

les œufs

le pain

la soupe

les légumes

le café

le sandwich

le lait

la pomme

l'orangeade

la glace

CONVERSATION

Bonsoir, mademoiselle. Voici le menu.

Merci. J'ai très faim. Il y a du jambon?

Certainement. Voulez-vous des pommes de terre avec la viande?

C'est ça. Et j'aimerais une salade aussi.

Très bien. Qu'est-ce que vous voulez boire?

Un cola.

Bon. Et comme dessert?

Une glace au chocolat, s'il vous plaît.

VOCABULAIRE

bonsoir *good evening*
j'ai très faim *I'm very hungry*
voulez-vous *do you want*
boire *to drink*

DIALOGUE

You are the second person in the dialog. Write an original response to each dialog line following the cues provided:

Bonsoir, monsieur. Voici le menu.

_____
(Say thank you and say what you want.)

Mais oui. Voulez-vous des pommes de terre avec la viande?

_____
(Say yes. Tell what else you would like.)

Très bien. Qu'est-ce que vous voulez boire?

_____
(Tell what.)

Bon. Et comme dessert?

_____
(Tell what.)

QUESTIONS PERSONNELLES

1. Quand vous avez faim, que mangez-vous?

_____

2. Quand vous avez soif, qu'est-ce que vous aimez boire?

_____

3. Aimez-vous les fruits?

_____

4. Mangez-vous les légumes?

_____

5. Aimez-vous préparer les desserts?

_____

186

VOUS

You are shopping for your family. Make a shopping list of the things you would buy:

1. _____
2. _____
3. _____
4. _____
5. _____
6. _____
7. _____
8. _____
9. _____
10. _____

14 | Quelle heure est-il?

1 In this lesson you will learn to tell time. First let's review the numbers from 1 to 30.

Activités

A. Match each item in the left column with the correct numeral in the right column. Write the number and matching letter in the space provided:

1. quinze	**a.** 7	_____
2. trois	**b.** 16	_____
3. vingt	**c.** 13	_____
4. seize	**d.** 5	_____
5. cinq	**e.** 3	_____
6. deux	**f.** 2	_____
7. quatorze	**g.** 15	_____
8. neuf	**h.** 9	_____
9. treize	**i.** 4	_____
10. six	**j.** 6	_____
11. quatre	**k.** 14	_____
12. sept	**l.** 20	_____

B. Write these numbers in French:

1. 21 _____

2. 14 _____

3. 30 _____

188

4. 7 _____

5. 16 _____

6. 18 _____

7. 12 _____

8. 29 _____

9. 15 _____

10. 11 _____

2 Now you are ready to learn to tell time.

Quelle heure est-il?

Il est midi.
Il est minuit.

Il est une heure.

Il est deux heures.

Il est trois heures.

Il est quatre heures.

Il est cinq heures.

Now see if you can do the rest:

6:00 _____

7:00 _____

8:00 _____

9:00 _____

10:00 _____

11:00 _____

3 When telling time in French, how do you express "it is"? _____

How do you express the time? _____

Why is the spelling of "**heures**" different for "**Il est une heure**"? _____

_____

How do you express "noon"? _____

How do you express "midnight"? _____

For "noon" and "midnight," what word do you leave out? _____

4 Now study these:

Il est deux heures cinq.   **Il est deux heures moins cinq.**

Il est trois heures cinq.   **Il est trois heures moins cinq.**

Il est quatre heures cinq.   **Il est quatre heures moins cinq.**

190

Continue writing these times:

5:05 _____   4:55 _____

6:05 _____   5:55 _____

7:05 _____   6:55 _____

8:05 _____   7:55 _____

5   How smart are you? How would you say:

7:10 _____   6:50 _____

8:10 _____   7:50 _____

9:10 _____   8:50 _____

10:20 _____   9:40 _____

11:20 _____   10:40 _____

12:20 (noon) _____   11:40 _____

1:25 _____   12:35 _____

2:25 _____   1:35 _____

3:25 _____   2:35 _____

How do you express time after the hour? _____

What word must you include to express time before the hour? _____

How would you say:

3:17 _____   6:57 _____

4:23 _____   7:42 _____

5:06 _____   8:39 _____

6 Now study these:

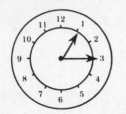

Il est une heure et quart.

Il est une heure moins le quart.

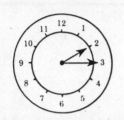

Il est deux heures et quart.

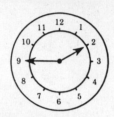

Il est deux heures moins le quart.

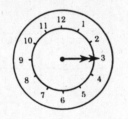

Il est trois heures et quart.

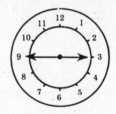

Il est trois heures moins le quart.

Il est quatre heures et quart.

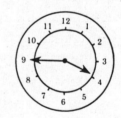

Il est quatre heures moins le quart.

How would you express:

5:15 _____

6:15 _____

7:15 _____

8:15 _____

4:45 _____

5:45 _____

192

6:45 _____

7:45 _____

What is the special word for "quarter"? _____

What little word do you add for "a quarter after?" _____

What little words do you add for "a quarter before the hour"? _____

7 Now study these:

Il est une heure et demie.

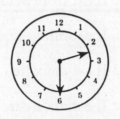

Il est deux heures et demie.

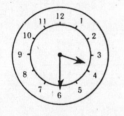

Il est trois heures et demie.

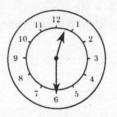

Il est midi et demi.
Il est minuit et demi.

How would you say:

4:30 _____

5:30 _____

6:30 _____

7:30 _____

What is the special word for "half past"? _____

What is the special spelling for "half past" when it is used with **midi** or

minuit? _____

What little word do you add to show that "half past" is after the hour?

_____

Activités

C. Write out these times in numbers:

EXAMPLE: **Il est une heure.**   **1:00**

1. Il est neuf heures moins le quart. _____

2. Il est six heures et demie.   _____

3. Il est quatre heures dix.   _____

4. Il est trois heures moins cinq.   _____

5. Il est midi et quart.   _____

6. Il est deux heures vingt.   _____

7. Il est dix heures moins dix.   _____

8. Il est onze heures moins vingt.   _____

9. Il est huit heures cinq.   _____

10. Il est une heure moins vingt-cinq. _____

D. Write these times in French:

1. 10:20 _____

2. 7:55 _____

3. 11:30 _____

4. 6:45 _____

5. 4:35 _____

6. 8:25 _____

7. 12:50 _____

8. 2:40 _____

9. 9:16 _____

10. 3:42 _____

E. Here are some clocks. What times does each one show?

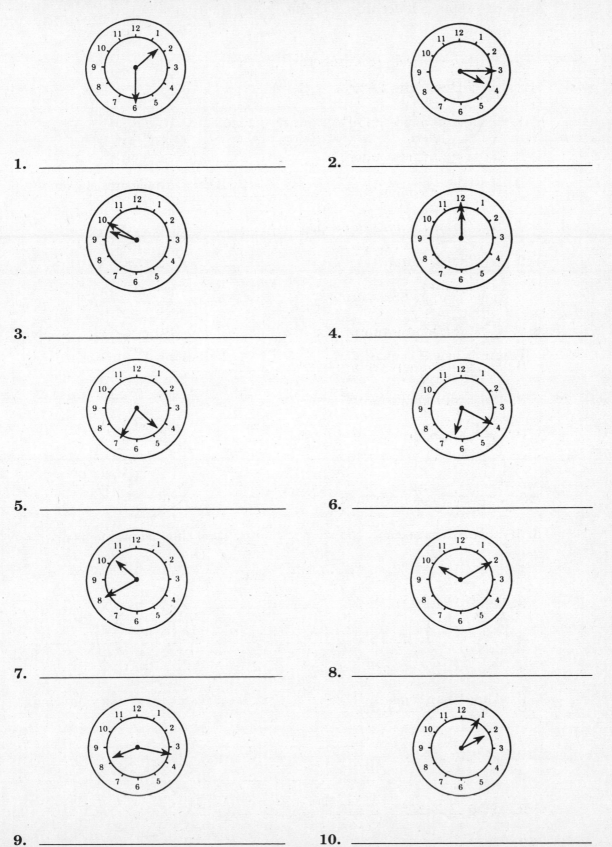

1. _____   2. _____

3. _____   4. _____

5. _____   6. _____

7. _____   8. _____

9. _____   10. _____

F. Here are some broken clocks. Each one has the minute hand missing. See if you can replace it according to the correct time:

1. Il est deux heures.

2. Il est quatre heures et demie.

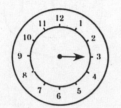

3. Il est trois heures et quart.

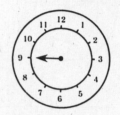

4. Il est neuf heures onze.

5. Il est onze heures cinq.

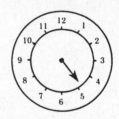

6. Il est cinq heures moins dix.

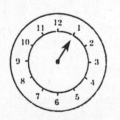

7. Il est une heure et quart.

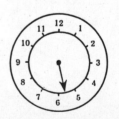

8. Il est six heures moins vingt-cinq.

9. Il est minuit.

10. Il est midi.

8 Look at the following questions and answers:

À quelle heure dînez-vous?   **Je dîne à six heures.**
À quelle heure préparez-vous les devoirs?   **Je prépare les devoirs à huit heures.**
À quelle heure regardez-vous la télé?   **Je regarde la télé à neuf heures.**

If you want to express "at" a certain time, what French word must you use

before the time? _____

Activités

G. Here are some daily activities. Tell at what time they occur:

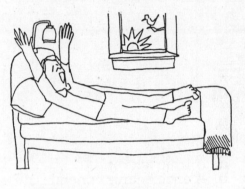

a. À une heure et demie.
b. À sept heures.
1. _____   c. À trois heures.

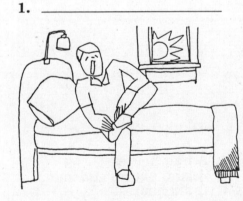

a. À neuf heures et demie.
b. À quatre heures.
2. _____   c. À sept heures et demie.

a. À huit heures dix.
b. À onze heures.
3. _____   c. À une heure et quart.

a. À sept heures.
b. À deux heures.
4. _____ c. À midi.

a. À trois heures.
b. À onze heures et demie.
5. _____ c. À deux heures moins vingt.

a. À huit heures.
b. À cinq heures et demie.
6. _____ c. À dix heures.

a. À deux heures et demie.
b. À cinq heures cinq.
7. _____ c. À huit heures moins cinq.

198

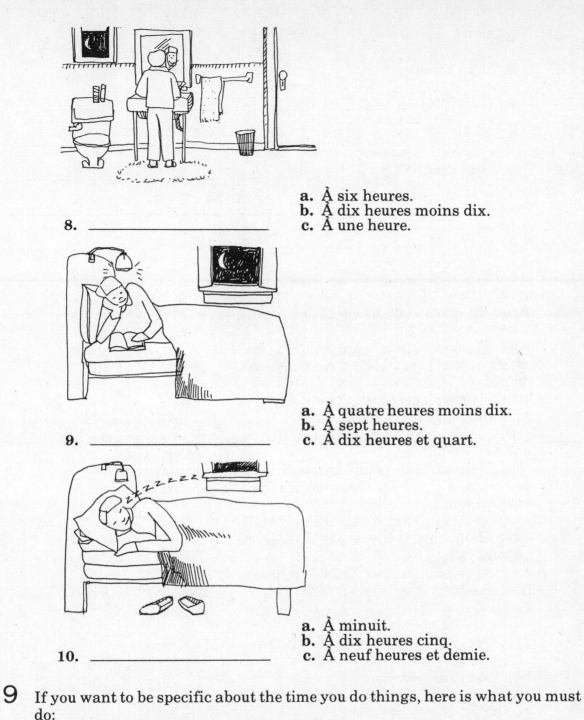

a. À six heures.
b. À dix heures moins dix.
c. À une heure.

8. _____

a. À quatre heures moins dix.
b. À sept heures.
c. À dix heures et quart.

9. _____

a. À minuit.
b. À dix heures cinq.
c. À neuf heures et demie.

10. _____

9 If you want to be specific about the time you do things, here is what you must do:

Je mange les flocons de maïs (*corn flakes*) **à huit heures** *du matin.*
Je mange un sandwich à une heure *de l'après-midi.*
Je mange le dîner à six heures *du soir.*

How do we express "in the morning" in French? _____

How do we express "in the afternoon"? _____

How do we express "in the evening"? _____

Activité

H. Write in French:

1. 11:35 P.M. _____

2. 3:15 A.M. _____

3. 4:45 P.M. _____

4. 9:57 A.M. _____

5. 8:23 P.M. _____

6. 2:14 P.M. _____

10 Read the story and answer the questions:

ANDRÉ: Maman, quelle heure est-il?
MAMAN: Écoute la radio! Il est neuf heures et demie.
ANDRÉ: Neuf heures et demie? Impossible. Il est huit heures dix à ma montre.
MAMAN: Ta montre ne marche pas. Achète une autre montre.
ANDRÉ: Oui, oui. Mais je suis en retard. Il y a un examen dans la classe de français aujourd'hui.
MAMAN: Il y a un examen aujourd'hui? Mais c'est dimanche. Il n'y a pas de classes aujourd'hui.
ANDRÉ: C'est dimanche? Quelle surprise! Dieu merci!

ma montre *my watch*
ta *your*   **marche** *work*
achète *buy*
en retard *late*
un examen *a test*

Dieu *God*   **merci** *thanks to*

Activité

I. Répondez aux questions:

1. Qui parle avec maman?

_____

2. Selon (*according to*) la montre d'André, quelle heure est-il?

_____

3. Selon la radio, quelle heure est-il?

_____

4. Dans quelle classe André a-t-il un examen?

_____

5. Pourquoi est-ce qu'il n'y a pas de classes aujourd'hui?

_____

QUESTIONS PERSONNELLES

1. Quelle heure est-il?

_____

2. À quelle heure mangez-vous le petit déjeuner?

_____

3. À quelle heure arrivez-vous à l'école?

_____

4. À quelle heure commence la classe de français?

_____

5. À quelle heure finissent les classes?

_____

6. À quelle heure quittez-vous l'école?

_____

7. À quelle heure dînez-vous?

_____

8. À quelle heure préparez-vous les devoirs?

_____

9. À quelle heure écoutez-vous la musique?

_____

10. À quelle heure regardez-vous la télévision?

_____

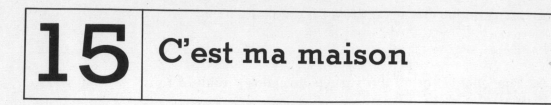

15 | C'est ma maison

1 Look at the pictures and try to guess the meanings of the new words:

la maison

la chambre

la cuisine

la salle à manger

la salle de bains

la télé

la radio

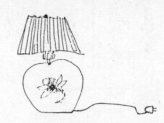

la lampe

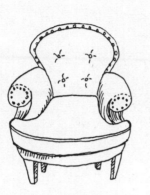

la chaise

le lit

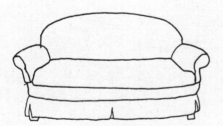

le divan

l'immeuble (*m.*)

l'appartement (*m.*)

l'étage (*m.*)

203

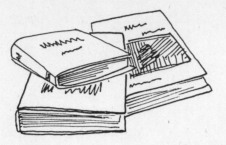

les livres

les disques

les photos

Activités

A. Qu'est-ce que c'est? Name the objects. Use articles:

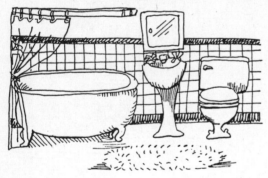

1. _____

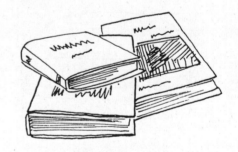

2. _____

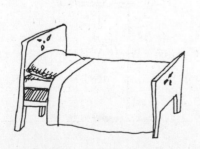

3. _____

4. _____

5. _____   6. _____

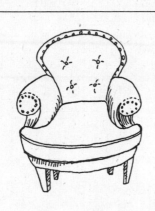

7. _____   8. _____

9. _____   10. _____

B. Finissez les phrases:

1. J'habite _____.

2. Je prépare les repas dans _____.

3. Je mange dans _____.

4. Je regarde la télé dans _____.

5. Dans ma chambre il y a _____.

2 In this chapter you are going to learn how to say that something belongs to someone. You will learn about *possession* and *possessive adjectives*. Pay special attention to each group of sentences:

I	II
C'est *le* lit.	C'est *mon* lit.
C'est *le* divan.	C'est *mon* divan.
C'est *le* livre.	C'est *mon* livre.

Look at the nouns in the first group of sentences. Underline them.

Are they masculine or feminine? _____ Singular or plural?

_____

How do you know? _____

Do they begin with consonants or vowels? _____

Now look at Group II. What word has replaced **le** from Group I? _____

What does **mon** mean? _____

Before what kinds of nouns is it used? _____

_____

3

I	II
C'est *la* chambre.	C'est *ma* chambre.
C'est *la* maison.	C'est *ma* maison.
C'est *la* cuisine.	C'est *ma* cuisine.

Look at the nouns in the first group of sentences. Underline them.

Are they masculine or feminine? _____ Singular or plural?

_____

How do you know? _____

Do they begin with consonants or vowels? _____

Now look at Group II. What word has replaced **la** from Group I? _____

What does **ma** mean? _____

Before what kinds of nouns is it used? _____

_____

206

4

I	II
C'est *l'*ami.	C'est *mon* ami.
C'est *l'*amie.	C'est *mon* amie.

Look at the nouns in Group I. Underline them. Are they masculine or feminine? _____ Singular or plural? _____ Do they begin with a consonant or vowel? _____

Now look at Group II. What possessive adjective is used before all singular nouns that start with a vowel? _____

5

I	II
Ce sont *les* disques.	Ce sont *mes* disques.
Ce sont *les* livres.	Ce sont *mes* livres.
Ce sont *les* photos.	Ce sont *mes* photos.
Ce sont *les* amis.	Ce sont *mes* amis.

Look at the nouns in the first group of sentences. Underline them.

Are they masculine or feminine? _____ Singular or plural? _____

How do you know? _____

Do they begin with consonants or vowels? _____

Now look at Group II. What word has replaced **les** from Group I? _____

What does **mes** mean? _____

Before what kinds of nouns is it used? _____

6 How many ways are there to say MY? _____

When do you use **mon?** _____

_____

ma? _____

mes? _____

Activité

C. Fill in **mon, ma,** or **mes:**

1. _____ mère   6. _____ dents

2. _____ livres   7. _____ bouche

3. _____ oncle   8. _____ disques

4. _____ amies   9. _____ télévision

5. _____ tête   10. _____ professeur

7 See if you can apply these rules to other possessive adjectives:

C'est *le* lit.   C'est *ton* lit.
C'est *la* chambre.   C'est *ta* chambre.
C'est *l'*amie.   C'est *ton* amie.
Ce sont *les* livres.   Ce sont *tes* livres.

What subject pronoun do **ton, ta,** and **tes** bring to mind? _____

What do **ton, ta,** and **tes** mean? _____

When do you use **ton?** _____

_____

ta? _____

tes? _____

When you use **ton, ta,** and **tes**, are you being familiar or formal? _____

Activité

D. Fill in the correct form of **ton, ta,** or **tes:**

1. _____ oreilles   6. _____ dents

2. _____ jambon   7. _____ bouche

3. _____ fruit   8. _____ amie

4. _____ argent   9. _____ nez

5. _____ salade   10. _____ yeux

8 Keeping in mind the rules you have already learned, look at the next group of possessive adjectives:

C'est *le lit de Paul.*   C'est *son lit.*
C'est *le lit de Marie.*   C'est *son lit.*

C'est *la chambre de Paul.*   C'est *sa chambre.*
C'est *la chambre de Marie.*   C'est *sa chambre.*

C'est *l'amie de Paul.*   C'est *son amie.*
C'est *l'amie de Marie.*   C'est *son amie.*

Ce sont *les livres de Paul.*   Ce sont *ses livres.*
Ce sont *les livres de Marie.*   Ce sont *ses livres.*

When do you use **son**? _____

_____

sa? _____

ses? _____

Son, sa, and **ses** have two meanings. What are they? _____

Does the possessive adjective **son, sa, ses** agree with the possessor or with the

thing he or she possesses? _____

Activités

E. Fill in the correct form of **son, sa,** or **ses:**

1. _____ doigts   6. _____ fenêtres

2. _____ estomac   7. _____ figure

3. _____ cahier   8. _____ classes

4. _____ mousse   9. _____ stylo

5. _____ dictionnaires   10. _____ bureau

F. Write in French:

1. his mother _____

2. her father _____

3. his aunts _____

4. her uncles _____

5. his pen _____

6. her book _____

7. his notebook _____

8. her hand _____

9. his sandwich _____

10. her sandwich _____

G. Choose the correct possessive adjective:

1. (mon, ma, mes) _____ famille

2. (ton, ta, tes) _____ étage

3. (son, sa, ses) _____ cahier

4. (mon, ma, mes) _____ immeubles

5. (ton, ta, tes) _____ lit

6. (son, sa, ses) _____ chambre

7. (mon, ma, mes) _____ professeurs

8. (ton, ta, tes) _____ école

9. (son, sa, ses) _____ cuisine

10. (mon, ma, mes) _____ maison

11. (ton, ta, tes) _____ devoirs

12. (son, sa, ses) _____ amie.

H. Fill in the correct possessive adjective:

1. (my) _____ amie

2. (your) _____ cahier

3. (his) _____ mère

4. (her) _____ frère

5. (my) _____ sandwich

6. (your) _____ oreilles

7. (his) _____ bouche

8. (her) _____ dents

9. (my) _____ jambes

10. (your) _____ cœur

11. (his) _____ télévision

12. (her) _____ sœur.

9 Let's learn some more about the possessive:

C'est *le* lit.   C'est *notre* lit.
C'est *la* chambre.   C'est *notre* chambre.
C'est *l'*amie.   C'est *notre* amie.
Ce sont *les* livres.   Ce sont *nos* livres.

What subject pronoun do **notre** and **nos** bring to mind? _____

What do **notre** and **nos** mean? _____

When do you use **notre?** _____

           nos? _____

C'est *le* lit.   C'est *votre* lit.
C'est *la* chambre.   C'est *votre* chambre.
C'est *l'*amie.   C'est *votre* amie.
Ce sont *les* livres.   Ce sont *vos* livres.

What subject pronoun do **votre** and **vos** bring to mind? _____

What do **votre** and **vos** mean? _____

When do you use **votre?** _____

           vos? _____

Are you being familiar or formal? _____

C'est *le* lit.   C'est leur lit.
C'est *la* chambre.   C'est *leur* chambre.
C'est *l'*amie.   C'est *leur* amie.
Ce sont *les* livres.   Ce sont *leurs* livres.

What do **leur** and **leurs** mean? _____

When do you use **leur?** _____

                    leurs? _____

Activité

I. Choose the correct possessive adjective:

1. (notre, nos) _____ classe.

2. (votre, vos) _____ crayons.

3. (leur, leurs) _____ famille.

4. (notre, nos) _____ cahiers.

5. (votre, vos) _____ main.

6. (leur, leurs) _____ chambres.

7. (notre, nos) _____ frère.

8. (votre, vos) _____ papiers.

9. (leur, leurs) _____ orangeade.

10 Read this story about two girls trying to impress each other:

JEANNE: Bonjour Sylvie. Ça va?   **Ça va?** *How's it going?*
SYLVIE: Ça va. Il y a beaucoup de travail.   **Ça va** *O.K.*
JEANNE: Beaucoup de travail? Pourquoi?   **travail** *work*
SYLVIE: Notre famille habite une grande
    maison. Il y a beaucoup de chambres dans
    notre maison. J'aide ma mère à faire le   **faire le ménage** *to do the*
    ménage.   *housework*
JEANNE: Oui, moi aussi. Ma maison est
    énorme aussi. Nous avons dix pièces. Mes   **pièces** *rooms*
    parents ont une grande chambre. Ma
    sœur et moi, nous avons une grande
    chambre et mon frère a une grande
    chambre aussi.

212

SYLVIE: Combien de salles de bains avez-vous?

JEANNE: Deux. Mais nous avons aussi un grand salon, une salle à manger et une cuisine où notre bonne prépare les repas.

SYLVIE: Oui, notre bonne prépare et sert les repas aussi. (À ce moment-là la mère de Sylvie entre.)

MAMAN (seule avec sa fille): Sylvie, pourquoi dis-tu que nous avons une bonne? Tu sais bien que ce n'est pas vrai.

SYLVIE: Oui, maman. Nous parlons peut-être trop. Jeanne habite comme nous un petit appartement.

où *where*   **la bonne** *the maid*
le repas *the meal*   **sert** *serves*

seule *alone*   **dis-tu** *do you say*
tu sais bien *you know well*
ce n'est pas vrai *it's not true*

peut-être *perhaps*

Activité

J. Finissez les phrases:

1. Selon Sylvie, sa famille habite _____.

2. Dans la maison il y a beaucoup de _____.

3. Sylvie aide sa mère à _____.

4. Selon Jeanne, sa maison est _____.

5. La maison de Jeanne a _____ pièces.

6. Ses parents ont _____.

7. La maison de Jeanne a deux _____.

8. _____ prépare les repas.

9. Elle prépare les repas dans _____.

10. À vrai dire (*Really*), Sylvie et Jeanne habitent _____.

QUESTIONS PERSONNELLES

1. Où est votre lit?

_____

2. Où préparez-vous le dîner?

_____

3. Où regardez-vous la télévision?

_____

4. Comment est votre maison?

_____

5. Combien d'étages a votre maison?

_____

VOUS

Draw your house and especially your room. Label the rooms in your house and the objects in your room.

16 | Le couvert

1 Look at the pictures and try to guess the meanings of the new words:

le couvert

la nappe

la serviette

la cuiller

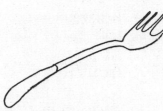

la fourchette

la tasse

l'addition

l'assiette

le couteau

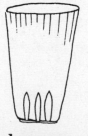

le verre

le menu

le pourboire

215

le restaurant

le petit déjeuner

le déjeuner

le dîner

le garçon

la serveuse

Activités

A. Fill in the correct definite article **le, la,** or **les:**

1. _____ couteau   2. _____ serviette

3. _____ restaurants   4. _____ addition

5. _____ menu   6. _____ dîners

7. _____ nappe   8. _____ fourchette

9. _____ tasses   10. _____ petit déjeuner

11. _____ pourboire   12. _____ cuiller

B. Identifiez:

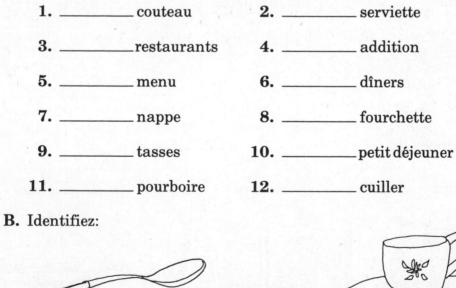

1. _____   2. _____

216

3. _____

4. _____

5. _____

6. _____

7. _____

8. _____

9. _____

10. _____

C. Mettez le couvert et identifiez les choses (*Set the table and identify the objects*):

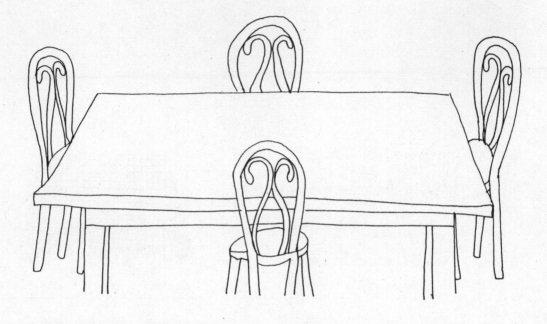

2 Read the story and answer the questions about it:

Nous sommes en été. Il fait très chaud. Mme Leblanc ne veut pas préparer le dîner. Alors, la famille Leblanc décide de dîner dans un restaurant élégant. La famille arrive au restaurant «Chez Claude» et va à une grande table près de la fenêtre. Le garçon donne un menu à chaque membre de la famille. M. et Mme Leblanc, Janine et Paul regardent la table et ils se mettent à rire. Voici ce qu'ils voient:

l'été *the summer*
  il fait chaud *it's hot*

près de *near*
chaque *each*

se mettent à *begin to*
rire *laugh*   **voient** *see*

Papa Leblanc appelle le garçon et dit: Qui a mis le couvert? Le garçon regarde la table et il se met à rire aussi. Il dit: «Le fils de M. Claude a mis le couvert pour aider son père le propriétaire. Il a seulement cinq ans et il n'est pas très sérieux. Il veut un pourboire. Je vais tout arranger.»

Qui a mis le couvert? *Who set the table?*

le propriétaire *the boss*
  il a cinq ans *he is 5 years old*

Activités

D. Répondez aux questions:

1. En quelle saison sommes-nous?

   _____

2. Pourquoi la famille Leblanc dîne-t-elle au restaurant?

   _____

3. Qu'est-ce que le garçon donne à chaque membre de la famille?

   _____

4. Qui a mis le couvert?

   _____

5. Pourquoi?

   _____

E. Regardez le dessin de la table. Pourquoi est-ce que tout le monde (*everyone*) se met à rire? Donnez 5 raisons (*reasons*):

1. _____

2. _____

3. _____

4. _____

5. _____

3 In French there are many kinds of adjectives. Now you are going to learn about demonstrative adjectives. Look at the two groups of words:

I	II
la nappe	*cette* nappe
la serviette	*cette* serviette
la serveuse	*cette* serveuse
la fourchette	*cette* fourchette
la tasse	*cette* tasse
l'assiette	*cette* assiette

What is the gender of all of these words? _____

Are they singular or plural? _____

How do you know? _____

What word in Group II replaces **la** from Group I? _____

What does **cette** mean? _____

Is **cette** used with nouns that start with consonants or vowels? _____

4

I	II
le couteau	*ce* couteau
le verre	*ce* verre
le menu	*ce* menu
le restaurant	*ce* restaurant
le pourboire	*ce* pourboire

What is the gender of all of these words? _____

Are they singular or plural? _____

How do you know? _____

What word in Group II replaces **le** from Group I? _____

What does **ce** mean? _____

Is it used with nouns that start with consonants or vowels? _____

5

I	II
l'homme	*cet* homme
l'ami	*cet* ami
l'enfant *m.*	*cet* enfant
l'élève *m.*	*cet* élève

What is the gender of all of these words? _____

Are they singular or plural? _____

How do you know? _____

What word in Group II replaces l' from Group I? _____

What does **cet** mean? _____

Is **cet** used with nouns that start with consonants or vowels? _____

6

I	II
les nappes	*ces* nappes
les menus	*ces* menus
les hommes	*ces* hommes
les serviettes	*ces* serviettes
les restaurants	*ces* restaurants
les amis	*ces* amis

What is the gender of all of these words? _____

Are they singular or plural? _____

How do you know? _____

What word in Group II replaces **les** from Group I? _____

What does **ces** mean? _____

Is **ces** used with nouns that start with consonants or vowels? _____

7   Summary

Cette, cet, ce all mean _____. **Ces** means _____.

Use **cette** before _____

    cet _____

    ce _____

    ces _____

221

Activités

F. Fill in the correct demonstrative adjective **cette, cet, ce, ces:**

1. _____ verres   2. _____ homme

3. _____ restaurant   4. _____ carte

5. _____ oncles   6. _____ assiette

7. _____ garçons   8. _____ pourboire

9. _____ addition   10. _____ nappe

11. _____ fourchette   12. _____ enfants

13. _____ déjeuner   14. _____ élève

15. _____ dîner   16. _____ famille

G. Fill in the correct demonstrative adjective:

1. (this) _____ hôtel   2. (that) _____ fenêtre

3. (these) _____ stylos   4. (those) _____ fromages

5. (these) _____ cafés   6. (that) _____ orangeade

7. (those) _____ bras   8. (this) _____ coeur

9. (that) _____ amie   10. (those) _____ portes

11. (this) _____ argent   12. (these) _____ professeurs

13. (those) _____ écoles   14. (this) _____ lit

15. (that) _____ immeuble   16. (these) _____ maisons

QUESTIONS PERSONNELLES

1. Qu'est-ce que vous mangez pour le petit déjeuner?

_____

2. Qu'est-ce que vous mangez pour le déjeuner?

_____

3. Qu'est-ce que vous mangez pour le dîner?

_____

4. Qu'est-ce que vous donnez à la serveuse dans un restaurant?

_____

5. Avec quoi (*what*) mangez-vous la soupe?

_____

6. Avec quoi mangez-vous la viande, les légumes et la salade?

_____

Révision IV (Leçons 13-16)

Leçon 13

The partitive is used to express *some*, that is, part of a thing:

Use **du** before masculine singular nouns beginning with a consonant.
Use **de la** before feminine singular nouns beginning with a consonant.
Use **de l'** before masculine and feminine singular nouns beginning with a vowel.
Use **des** before all plural nouns.

Leçon 14

a. Time is expressed as follows:

Quelle heure est-il? *What time is it?*

Il est une heure.	1:00	**Il est sept heures et demie.**	7:30
Il est deux heures cinq.	2:05	**Il est huit heures moins vingt-cinq.**	7:35
Il est trois heures dix.	3:10	**Il est neuf heures moins vingt.**	8:40
Il est quatre heures et quart.	4:15	**Il est dix heures moins le quart.**	9:45
Il est cinq heures vingt.	5:20	**Il est onze heures moins dix.**	10:50
Il est six heures vingt-cinq.	6:25	**Il est midi moins cinq.**	11:55 (noon)
		Il est minuit.	midnight

b. To express "at" a specific time, use **à**:

À quelle heure mangez-vous? Je mange *à* six heures.

Leçon 15

The possessive is used to show that something belongs to someone:

Use **mon**	(*my*)	
ton	(*your*)	Before masculine singular nouns beginning with a consonant.
son	(*his, her, its*)	
notre	(*our*)	Before all singular nouns beginning with a vowel.
votre	(*your*)	
leur	(*their*)	

224

Use **ma** (*my*)
    ta (*your*)
    sa (*his, her, its*)   Before feminine singular nouns beginning
    notre (*our*)   with a consonant.
    votre (*your*)
    leur (*their*)

Use **mes** (*my*)
    tes (*your*)
    ses (*his, her, its*)   Before ALL plural nouns.
    nos (*our*)
    vos (*your*)
    leurs (*their*)

Leçon 16

Demonstrative adjectives are used to express *this, that* or *these, those*:

Use **ce** before masculine singular nouns beginning with a consonant to express *this/that*.

Use **cet** before masculine singular nouns beginning with a vowel to express *this/that*.

Use **cette** before all feminine singular nouns to express *this/that*.

Use **ces** before all plural nouns to express *these/those*.

Activités

A. Write the French word under the picture you see. Then find the French word in the puzzle on page 227:

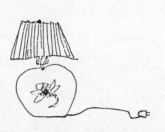 

1. _____   2. _____

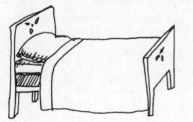 

3. _____   4. _____

5. _____

6. _____

7. _____

8. _____

9. _____

10. _____

11. _____

12. _____

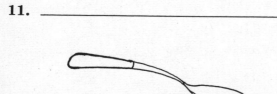

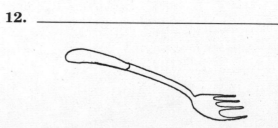

13. _____

14. _____

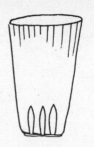

15. _____   16. _____

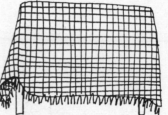

17. _____   18. _____

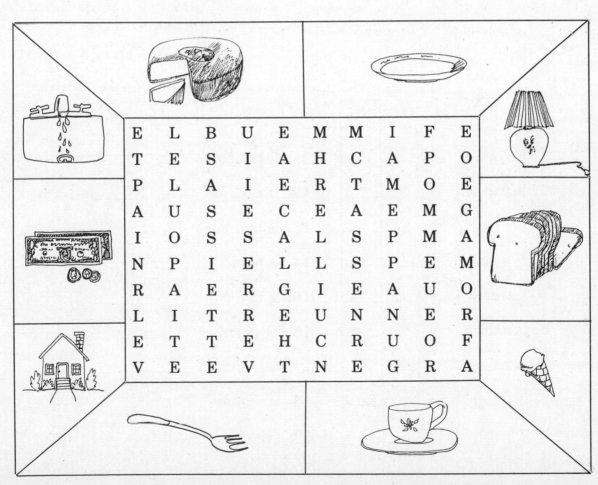

E	L	B	U	E	M	M	I	F	E
T	E	S	I	A	H	C	A	P	O
P	L	A	I	E	R	T	M	O	E
A	U	S	E	C	A	E	M	M	G
I	O	S	S	A	L	S	P	M	A
N	P	I	E	L	L	S	P	E	M
R	A	E	R	G	I	E	A	U	O
L	I	T	R	E	U	N	N	E	R
E	T	T	E	H	C	R	U	O	F
V	E	E	V	T	N	E	G	R	A

B. Pierre has just served a meal in a restaurant. But he has forgotten a few things. Can you help him out and check to see if the following items or foods are on the table?

	Oui	Non
1. les œufs		
2. le poisson		
3. la glace		
4. la soupe		
5. les oranges		
6. la salade		
7. la cuiller		
8. le fromage		
9. un verre		
10. le poulet		

	Oui	Non
11. le jambon		
12. le café		
13. le thon		
14. le pain		
15. le vin		
16. les pommes		
17. les fruits		
18. la viande		
19. l'eau		
20. la mousse		

C. Write the time in French:

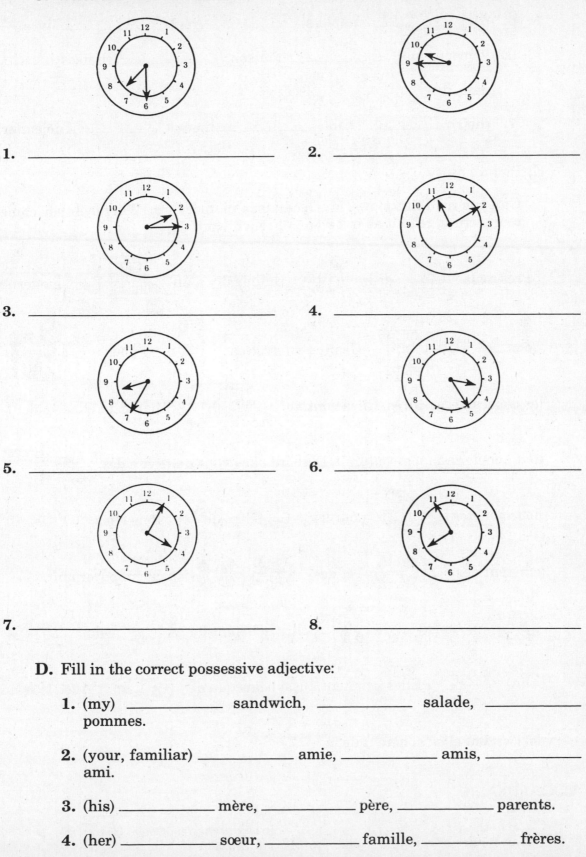

1. _____   2. _____

3. _____   4. _____

5. _____   6. _____

7. _____   8. _____

D. Fill in the correct possessive adjective:

1. (my) _____ sandwich, _____ salade, _____ pommes.

2. (your, familiar) _____ amie, _____ amis, _____ ami.

3. (his) _____ mère, _____ père, _____ parents.

4. (her) _____ sœur, _____ famille, _____ frères.

229

5. (our) _____ papiers, _____ règle, _____ livre.

6. (your, formal) _____ maison, _____ chaises, _____ lit.

7. (their) _____ table, _____ menus, _____ déjeuner.

E. Picture Story

Can you read this story? Much of it is in picture form. Whenever you come to a picture, read it as if it were a French word:

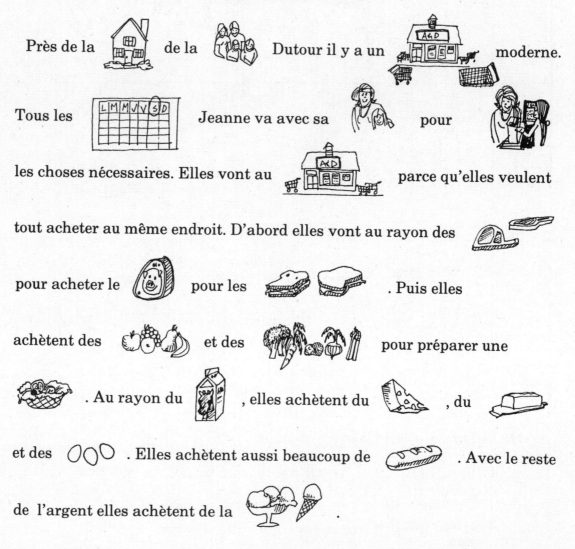

Près de la [maison] de la [famille] Dutour il y a un [supermarché] moderne. Tous les [semaines] Jeanne va avec sa [mère] pour [acheter] les choses nécessaires. Elles vont au [supermarché] parce qu'elles veulent tout acheter au même endroit. D'abord elles vont au rayon des [viandes] pour acheter le [jambon] pour les [sandwiches]. Puis elles achètent des [fruits] et des [légumes] pour préparer une [salade]. Au rayon du [lait], elles achètent du [fromage], du [beurre] et des [œufs]. Elles achètent aussi beaucoup de [pain]. Avec le reste de l'argent elles achètent de la [glace].

VOCABULAIRE

acheter *to buy*
au même endroit *at the same place*

le rayon *the department* (*in a store*)
puis *then*

230

Cinquième Partie

17 | Les numéros

40 **quarante**
50 **cinquante**
60 **soixante**
70 **soixante-dix**   80 **quatre-vingts**   90 **quatre-vingt-dix**
71 **soixante et onze**   81 **quatre-vingt-un**   91 **quatre-vingt-onze**
72 **soixante-douze**   82 **quatre-vingt-deux**   92 **quatre-vingt-douze**

73 **soixante-treize**   83 **quatre-vingt-trois**   93 **quatre-vingt-treize**

74 **soixante-quatorze**   84 **quatre-vingt-quatre**   94 **quatre-vingt-quatorze**

75 **soixante-quinze**   85 **quatre-vingt-cinq**   95 **quatre-vingt-quinze**

76 **soixante-seize**   86 **quatre-vingt-six**   96 **quatre-vingt-seize**

77 **soixante-dix-sept**   87 **quatre-vingt-sept**   97 **quatre-vingt-dix-sept**

78 **soixante-dix-huit**   88 **quatre-vingt-huit**   98 **quatre-vingt-dix-huit**

79 **soixante-dix-neuf**   89 **quatre-vingt-neuf**   99 **quatre-vingt-dix-neuf**
                                                          100 **cent**

Activités

A. Read the following numbers aloud and place the correct numeral in the spaces provided:

1. vingt-cinq _____   2. soixante-huit _____

3. quarante-neuf _____   4. seize _____

5. trente-deux _____   6. cinquante-six _____

7. quinze _____   8. treize _____

9. douze _____   10. quatorze _____

11. onze _____   12. dix-sept _____

B. You have seen that the numbers from 70-99 are tricky. See if you can recognize these numbers and write the numerals in the spaces provided:

1. quatre-vingts   _____

2. soixante-dix   _____

3. quatre-vingt-cinq _____

4. quatre-vingt-quinze _____

5. soixante et un   _____

6. soixante et onze   _____

7. quatre-vingt-seize _____

8. soixante-six   _____

9. quatre-vingt-neuf _____

10. soixante-quatorze _____

C. Match the list of French numbers with the numerals. Write the number and matching letter in the space provided:

1. quatre-vingt-treize   **a.** 63   _____

2. quarante-sept   **b.** 59   _____

3. soixante-douze   **c.** 28   _____

4. vingt-huit   **d.** 34   _____

5. cinquante-neuf   **e.** 93   _____

6. soixante-trois   **f.** 100   _____

7. trente-quatre   **g.** 47   _____

8. quatre-vingt-trois   **h.** 13   _____

9. cent   **i.** 72   _____

10. treize   **j.** 83   _____

1 Here is a story about an auction. Auctions can be fun, but be careful. Read the story and then answer the questions about it:

VENDEUR: Voici un tableau exceptionnel. C'est l'œuvre d'un artiste très célèbre, Paul Soupe de Poisson. Le tableau s'appelle «Le chien qui mange du gâteau dans son lit».

TOUT LE MONDE: Aaaaah!

ANDRÉ: Il est horrible.

SYLVIE: Il est monstrueux.

VENDEUR: Bon. Combien offrez-vous pour ce tableau extraordinaire? Qui me donne cinquante dollars?

ACHETEUR #1: Cinquante dollars.

l'œuvre *the work*
célèbre *famous*
s'appelle *is called*

ACHETEUR #2: Soixante dollars.

ANDRÉ: Ils sont fous.

SYLVIE: Ce tableau ne vaut pas cinquante centimes.

fous *crazy*
vaut *is worth*
centimes *cents*
affreux *terrible*

ANDRÉ: Ce tableau est affreux.

ACHETEUR #1: Soixante-dix dollars.

ACHETEUR #2: Quatre-vingts dollars.

ACHETEUR #1: Quatre-vingt-dix dollars.

VENDEUR: Quatre-vingt-dix dollars une fois, quatre-vingt-dix dollars deux fois . . . (À ce moment-là Régine entre.) Est-ce que j'entends cent dollars?

RÉGINE: Tiens! Sylvie, ça va?

SYLVIE: (Elle lève la main pour saluer son amie.)

Tiens! *Well!, Hey!*
lève *raises*   **saluer** *to greet*

VENDEUR: Cent dollars—pour la demoiselle en rouge. Ce tableau est à elle.

la demoiselle *the young lady*
est à elle *belongs to her*

Activités

D. Répondez aux questions:

1. Qui est l'artiste?

_____

2. Quel est le titre (*title*) du tableau?

_____

3. Que pense André du tableau?

_____

4. Que pense Sylvie du tableau?

_____

5. Combien de personnes veulent acheter le tableau?

_____

6. Combien est-ce que Sylvie paie le tableau?

_____

E. Arithmetic in French. Can you solve these problems?

1. Add:

vingt	quarante	quatre-vingt-dix
+ trente	+ soixante	+ dix
————	————	————

2. Subtract:

quinze	douze	quatorze
− cinq	− onze	− un
————	————	————

3. Multiply:

cinq	onze	trente
× quatre	× huit	× trois
————	————	————

4. Divide:

quatre-vingts	seize	vingt-cinq
÷ quatre	÷ deux	÷ cinq
————	————	————

F. Rearrange the following list of numbers so that they are in order, the smallest first, the largest last:

1. quatre-vingt-dix _____

2. quinze _____

3. un _____

4. neuf _____

5. soixante _____

6. trente-quatre _____

7. seize _____

8. vingt-deux _____

9. soixante-dix _____

10. cent trois _____

236

G. Write these numbers in French:

1. 16 _____
2. 4 _____
3. 77 _____
4. 83 _____
5. 14 _____
6. 69 _____
7. 47 _____
8. 31 _____
9. 26 _____
10. 98 _____
11. 52 _____
12. 115 _____
13. 13 _____
14. 72 _____
15. 91 _____

QUESTIONS PERSONNELLES

1. Combien de livres avez-vous?

_____

2. Combien d'élèves sont dans votre classe de français?

_____

3. Votre grand-mère (grand-père), quel âge a-t-elle (a-t-il)?

_____

4. Votre chien, quel âge a-t-il?

_____

5. Combien de leçons a ce livre?

_____

VOUS

1. Write 6 different math problems in French:

_____

_____

_____

_____

_____

_____

2. Write these numbers in French:

a. the grade on your last French test _____

b. the number of presents you got for your birthday _____

c. the number of students in your gym class _____

d. the number of teachers in your school _____

18 | Les lieux

1 Can you guess the meanings of these new words?

la ville

la bibliothèque

la gare

l'aéroport

l'appartement

l'usine

l'hôtel

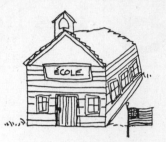

l'école

l'église

la piscine

le lycée

le restaurant

le musée

le village

le café

le théâtre

le cinéma

le match

le jardin

le château

Activités

A. Qu'est-ce que c'est?

1. _____

2. _____

3. _____

4. _____

5. _____

6. _____

B. Give the correct definite article **le, la, l', les**:

1. _____ gare

2. _____ aéroport

3. _____ hôtel

4. _____ musée

5. _____ restaurant

6. _____ bibliothèque

7. _____ chambre

8. _____ usine

9. _____ cuisine

10. _____ village

C. Identifiez:

1. _____

2. _____

3. _____

4. _____

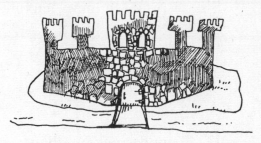

5. _____

6. _____

7. _____

8. _____

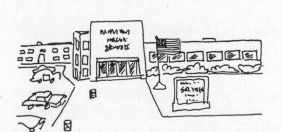

9. _____

10. _____

243

2 Now read this letter and see if you can answer the questions about it:

Paris, le 11 juillet

Chère maman,

J'adore Paris. Cette ville est très grande et belle. L'aéroport d'Orly est magnifique. J'habite l'Hôtel Madison. Ma chambre est petite. Je vais visiter Paris—tous les monuments, le musée du Louvre, la cathédrale de Notre Dame, le château de Versailles et le jardin des Tuileries. Je vais prendre mes repas dans des cafés et des restaurants célèbres. Mes vacances sont fantastiques. S'il te plaît, maman, envoie-moi encore $150. Merci.

vais *am going*   **tous** *all of*

Mes vacances *my vacation*
S'il te plaît *please*
    envoie *send*

Ta fille, Lisette

Activité

D. Répondez aux questions:

1. Qui est Lisette?

   _____

2. Qu'est-ce qu'elle adore?

   _____

3. Quelle est la date?

   _____

4. Que pense-t-elle de Paris?

   _____

5. Comment s'appelle (*What is the name of*) l'aéroport à Paris?

   _____

6. Quel hôtel Lisette habite-t-elle?

   _____

7. Qu'est-ce qu'elle va visiter?

   _____

8. Où va-t-elle prendre ses repas?

_____

9. Qu'est-ce qu'elle demande à sa maman?

_____

3   Now let's learn about French contractions. Look carefully at the groups of sentences:

I	II
J'arrive *à la* cuisine.	Je parle *de la* cuisine.
J'arrive *à la* chambre.	Je parle *de la* chambre.
J'arrive *à la* maison.	Je parle *de la* maison.
J'arrive *à la* ville.	Je parle *de la* ville.
J'arrive *à la* salle.	Je parle *de la* salle.

What is the gender of all of the nouns in Groups I and II? _____

Are the nouns singular or plural? _____

How do you know? _____

Do the nouns start with consonants or vowels? _____

What little word did we put before **la** in Group I? _____

What does **à la** mean? _____

What little word did we put before **la** in Group II? _____

What does **de la** mean? _____

4 | J'arrive *à l'*aéroport. | Je parle *de l'*aéroport. |
    | J'arrive *à l'*appartement. | Je parle *de l'*appartement. |
    | J'arrive *à l'*usine. | Je parle *de l'*usine. |

What is the gender of all of the nouns in Groups I and II? _____

Are the nouns singular or plural? _____

How do you know? _____

Do the nouns start with consonants or vowels? _____

What little word did we put before **l'** in Group I? _____

What does **à l'** mean? _____

245

What little word did we put before **l'** in Group II? _____

What does **de l'** mean? _____

5 **J'arrive** *au* **lycée.**   **Je parle** *du* **lycée.**
   J'arrive *au* **restaurant.**   **Je parle** *du* **restaurant.**
   J'arrive *au* **musée.**   **Je parle** *du* **musée.**
   J'arrive *au* **village.**   **Je parle** *du* **village.**
   J'arrive *au* **café.**   **Je parle** *du* **café.**

What is the gender of all of the nouns in Groups I and II? _____

Are the nouns singular or plural? _____

How do you know? _____

Do the nouns start with consonants or vowels? _____

What two little words did we combine to get **au?** _____

What does **au** mean? _____

What two little words did we combine to get **du?** _____

What does **du** mean? _____

What is the English word used when we combine two words to get one?

_____

6 **Ils arrivent** *aux* **maisons.**   **Ils parlent** *des* **maisons.**
   Ils arrivent *aux* **aéroports.**   **Ils parlent** *des* **aéroports.**
   Ils arrivent *aux* **lycées.**   **Ils parlent** *des* **lycées.**

What is the gender of all of the nouns in Group I and II? _____

Are the nouns singular or plural? _____

How do you know? _____

Do the nouns start with consonants or vowels? _____

What two little words did we combine to get **aux?** _____

What does **aux** mean? _____

What two little words did we combine to get **des?** _____

What does **des** mean? _____

7 Summary

How many ways are there to say "TO THE"? _____

What are they? _____

When do you use **à la?** _____

à l'? _____

au? _____

aux? _____

How many ways are there to say "OF (ABOUT) THE"? _____

What are they? _____

When do you use **de la?** _____

de l'? _____

du? _____

des? _____

Activités

E. Fill in the correct form of **à la, à l', au, aux:**

1. _____ aéroport   2. _____ cafés

3. _____ théâtre   4. _____ piscine

5. _____ maison   6. _____ musée

7. _____ bibliothèque   8. _____ école

9. _____ hôtels   10. _____ parc

11. _____ église   12. _____ ville

F. Fill in the correct form of **de la, de l', du, des:**

1. _____ usine   2. _____ cinéma

3. _____ chambres   4. _____ château

5. _____ gare   6. _____ appartements

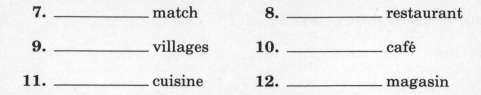

7. _____ match   8. _____ restaurant

9. _____ villages   10. _____ café

11. _____ cuisine   12. _____ magasin

QUESTIONS PERSONNELLES

1. Quel musée est célèbre?

_____

2. Quel restaurant aimez-vous?

_____

3. Où êtes-vous maintenant?

_____

4. De quoi (*About what*) parlez-vous avec vos amis?

_____

5. Où allez-vous prendre vos repas?

_____

VOUS

Name 5 places in French to which you go frequently:

Je vais

1. _____

2. _____

3. _____

4. _____

5. _____

19 Allons-y!

1 Can you guess the meanings of these new words?

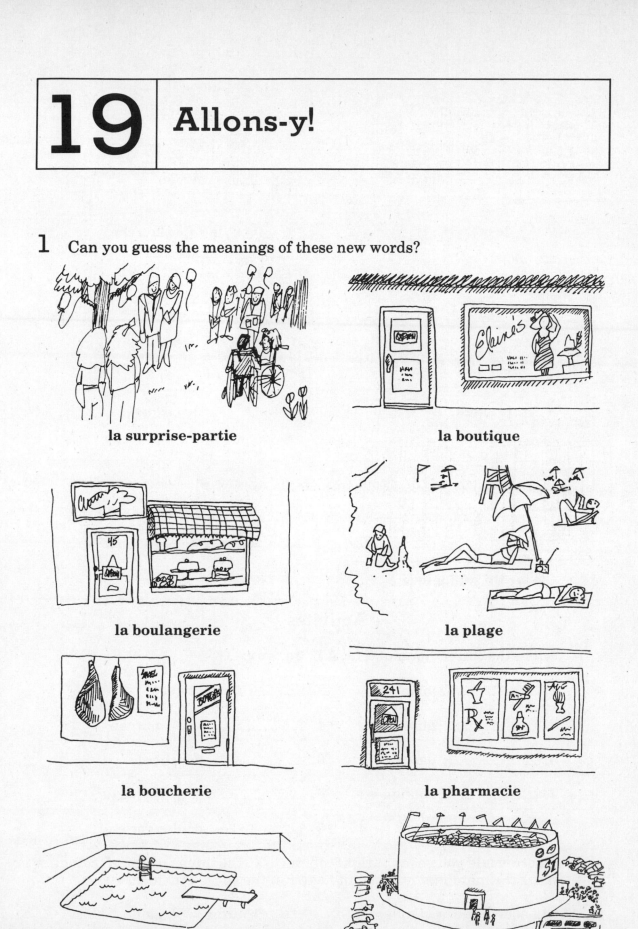

la surprise-partie

la boutique

la boulangerie

la plage

la boucherie

la pharmacie

la piscine

le stade

le marché

le supermarché

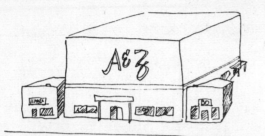

le magasin

le cirque

le jardin zoologique

le parc

Activités

A. Fill in the correct form of **à la, à l', au, aux:**

1. _____ magasins
2. _____ cirque
3. _____ plage
4. _____ supermarché
5. _____ parcs
6. _____ boucherie
7. _____ boutiques
8. _____ surprise-partie
9. _____ stade
10. _____ boulangerie

B. Where would you go in the right column to do the things in the left column? Write the matching number and letter in the space provided:

1. acheter de la viande   **a.** au jardin zoologique _____

2. nager   **b.** au supermarché _____

250

3. regarder les animaux   **c.** à la surprise-partie _____

4. acheter les aliments   **d.** au magasin _____

5. regarder un match   **e.** à la boucherie _____

6. acheter des gâteaux   **f.** au parc _____

7. acheter une jolie blouse   **g.** à la pharmacie _____

8. danser, manger, parler   **h.** au stade _____

9. acheter de l'aspirine   **i.** à la boulangerie _____

10. regarder les fleurs et les arbres   **j.** à la piscine _____

2   In the letter that follows are all the forms of the irregular French verb **aller** (*to go*). See if you can find them all:

Martinique, le 7 août

Chère Marie,

Comment vas-tu? **Je vais** bien. Je suis très contente parce que **je vais** tous les jours à la plage. Cet après-midi mon amie Danielle et moi, **nous allons** visiter tous les magasins de l'île. **Danielle va** être mon guide parce qu'elle visite la Martinique tout le temps. **Ses parents vont** acheter une maison sur cette île splendide.

après-midi *afternoon*

l'île *the island*
tout le temps *all the time*

Marie, **vas-tu** aller en vacances avec ta famille? Tes parents et toi, **allez-vous** en France? Quelle chance! Envoie-moi une carte postale.

Quelle chance *What luck*
Envoie-moi *Send me*

Ton amie Monique

Activité

C. Répondez aux questions:

1. Où Monique passe-t-elle ses vacances?

_____

2. Comment va-t-elle?

_____

3. Où va-t-elle cet après-midi?

_____

4. Avec qui?

_____

5. Qu'est-ce qu'elles vont visiter?

_____

6. Qui va être le guide?

_____

7. Qu'est-ce que les parents de Danielle vont acheter?

_____

8. Pourquoi?

_____

9. Où est-ce que Marie va en vacances?

_____

10. Avec qui?

_____

3 Did you find the forms of the irregular verbs **aller** in the story? Remember: **aller** is a special verb because it is one of a kind. No other verb in French is conjugated like **aller. Aller** means *to go*. Fill in the proper verb forms for each subject. MEMORIZE them:

je _____   nous _____

tu _____   vous _____

il _____   ils _____

elle _____   elles _____

4 Look carefully at these sentences from the letter:

Comment *vas-tu*?   *Je vais* bien.

The verb **aller** is used to express a person's _____.

5 Now look at these sentences from the story:

Nous allons visiter tous les magasins.
Danielle va être mon guide.
Ses parents vont acheter une maison.

When are these actions taking place? In the past? present? or future? _____

How do you know? _____

Underline the subject of each sentence. Now underline the verbs.

How many subjects are there in each sentence? _____

How many verbs are there? _____

Which verb is conjugated? _____

In what form is the second verb? _____

How do we form the near future in French? _____

_____

Why is it called the near future? _____

6 Now look at these sentences:

Nous *n*'allons *pas* visiter tous les magasins.
Danielle *ne* va *pas* être mon guide.
Ses parents *ne* vont *pas* acheter une maison.

How do we make a sentence containing a SUBJECT + CONJUGATED VERB + INFINITIVE negative?

_____

7 Now look at these sentences:

Allons-nous visiter tous les magasins?
Danielle *va-t-elle* être mon guide?
Ses parents *vont-ils* acheter une maison?

How do we make a sentence containing a SUBJECT + CONJUGATED VERB + INFINITIVE into a question using inversion?

_____

NOTE: Did you notice the title of this lesson? **Allons-y!** is an expression formed from the verb **aller**, and it has a special meaning: "Let's go!" "Let's get going!" "Let's do it!" "Let's get at it!"

Activités

D. Fill in the correct form of the verb **aller:**

1. Je ne _____ pas à l'école.

2. Nous _____ à l'aéroport.

3. _____ -vous à la surprise-partie?

4. Pierre _____ au supermarché.

5. Elle ne _____ pas à Paris.

6. Tu _____ au cinéma.

7. _____ -ils à la Martinique?

8. Je _____ au magasin.

9. Paul et Anne ne _____ pas à la boucherie.

10. Où _____ -t-il?

E. Make the following sentences negative:

1. Il va aller à la maison.

   _____

2. Vous allez visiter la cathédrale.

   _____

3. Tu vas écouter le disque.

   _____

4. Nous allons finir l'exercice.

   _____

5. Elles vont travailler à l'hôpital.

   _____

6. Pierre va être content.

   _____

7. Les professeurs vont parler en classe.

_____

8. Les femmes vont vendre les blouses.

_____

F. Change the sentences in Exercise E to questions using inversion:

1. _____

2. _____

3. _____

4. _____

5. _____

6. _____

7. _____

8. _____

G. Write in French:

1. (I am going to see)

_____ mes grands-parents.

2. (They are not going to sing.)

_____

3. (She is going to dance.)

_____

4. (You [familiar] are going to go)

_____ à Paris.

5. (We are going to work.)

_____

6. (Are you [formal] going to play?)

_____

7. (He is not going to finish.)

_____

8. (Are they going to sell?)

_____ la maison?

H. Using forms of the verb **aller,** describe what you see in the pictures:

1. _____ **2.** _____

3. _____ **4.** _____

5. _____ **6.** _____

7. _____ **8.** _____

CONVERSATION

Bonjour, madame.

Bonjour, Pierre. Qu'est-ce que vous avez comme fruits?

Eh bien . . . des pommes et des oranges.

Donnez-moi une douzaine de pommes.

Très bien, madame. Désirez-vous autre chose?

Eh bien . . . un pain, du lait et du fromage.

Voulez-vous aussi de la viande?

Non, merci. C'est tout. Ça fait combien?

VOCABULAIRE

une douzaine de *a dozen*
autre chose *something else*

ça fait combien? *that's how much?*

DIALOGUE

Rearrange the lines of dialog so that they are in a logical order. Write them in the correct order below:

1. Eh bien . . . des pommes et des oranges.
2. Voulez-vous aussi de la viande?
3. Bonjour, madame.
4. Très bien, madame. Désirez-vous autre chose?

      a. Non merci. C'est tout. Ça fait combien?
      b. Eh bien . . . du pain, du lait et du fromage.
      c. Donnez-moi une douzaine de pommes.
      d. Bonjour, Pierre. Qu'est-ce que vous avez comme fruits?

_____

_____

_____

_____

_____

_____

_____

QUESTIONS PERSONNELLES

1. Comment allez-vous?

_____

2. Pourquoi allez-vous à l'école?

_____

3. Avec qui allez-vous au cinéma?

_____

4. Où allez-vous après l'école?

_____

5. Quand allez-vous à la plage?

_____

6. Où allez-vous regarder un match?

_____

7. Où allez-vous chercher un livre?

_____

8. En quelle saison allez-vous à la piscine?

_____

9. Pour quelle raison allez-vous au restaurant?

_____

10. Avec quoi mangez-vous vos repas?

_____

VOUS

You have a lot of chores to do. Look at the clues and write a list of where you are going and why:

Où allez-vous?

1. Je vais _____

2. _____

3. _____

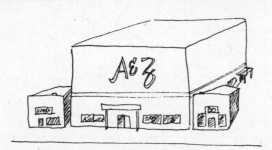

4. _____

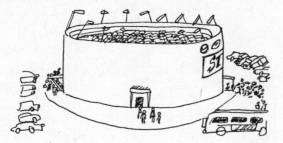

5. _____

6. _____

20 Quel temps fait-il?

1 Quel temps fait-il?

C'est le printemps.
Il fait beau.
Il fait du vent.

C'est l'été.
Il fait chaud.
Il fait du soleil.

C'est l'automne.
Il fait mauvais.
Il pleut.

C'est l'hiver.
Il fait froid.
Il neige.

Activité

A. Quel temps fait-il?

1. _____   2. _____

3. _____   4. _____

5. _____   6. _____

7. _____   8. _____

2 In the story that follows, all the forms of the irregular verb **faire** (*to make, to do*) appear. See if you can find them all:

Quand **il fait** chaud **je ne fais pas** mes devoirs. Mes amis et moi, **nous faisons** une promenade au parc. Une fois arrivés au parc, **les garçons font** une partie de football et **les filles ne font rien.** Elles regardent les garçons. Après le match **nous faisons** un pique-nique et nous mangeons beaucoup.

mes devoirs *my homework*
une promenade *a walk*
une partie *a game*
rien *nothing*

Le lendemain matin, le professeur demande: «Pourquoi **fais-tu** tes devoirs en classe?» Et moi, je réponds: «Quand **il fait** chaud, **je ne fais pas** mes devoirs. Que **faites-vous** quand il fait chaud?» Alors le professeur répond: «Hélas, quand **il fait** chaud, je punis les élèves.»

le lendemain matin *the next morning*

hélas *alas*

262

Activité

B. Finissez les phrases:

1. Quand il fait chaud, l'étudiante ne fait pas _____.

2. Elle _____ avec ses amis.

3. Au parc, les garçons _____.

4. Au parc, les filles _____.

5. Après le match, les garçons et les filles _____.

6. Le lendemain le prof demande à l'élève: _____.

7. L'élève répond: _____.

8. Quand il fait chaud, le prof _____.

3 Did you find the forms of the irregular verb **faire** in the story? Remember: **faire** is a special verb because it is one of a kind. No other verb in French is conjugated like **faire**. **Faire** means *to make, to do*. Fill in the proper verb forms for each subject. MEMORIZE them:

je	_____	nous	_____
tu	_____	vous	_____
il	_____	ils	_____
elle	_____	elles	_____

4 Now look carefully at these sentences:

Il *fait* chaud. Il *fait* du vent.
Il *fait* froid. Il *fait* du soleil.

Faire is used to express most _____ conditions.

Activités

C. Fill in the correct forms of the verb **faire**:

1. Vous _____ attention.

2. Je _____ ma valise.

3. Il _____ chaud.

4. Nous _____ les devoirs.

5. Elles _____ leur pique-nique.

6. Tu _____ l'omelette.

7. Elle _____ la liste.

8. Ils _____ ce voyage.

D. Make all the sentences in Exercise C negative:

1. _____

2. _____

3. _____

4. _____

5. _____

6. _____

7. _____

8. _____

E. Change all the sentences in Exercise C to questions using inversion:

1. _____

2. _____

3. _____

4. _____

5. _____

6. _____

7. _____

8. _____

F. Match the following expressions of weather with the correct pictures:

Il fait du vent. Il neige.
Il fait du soleil. Il pleut.
Il fait froid. Il fait beau.
Il fait chaud. Il fait mauvais.

1. _____ 2. _____

3. _____ 4. _____

5. _____ 6. _____

7. _____ 8. _____

G. Il ya a quatre saisons. En quelle saison sommes-nous?

1. Cette saison est très belle. Il fait beau. Il y a beaucoup de fleurs au parc. Tout est vert. Les oiseaux chantent dans les arbres. Les gens ne portent pas beaucoup de vêtements. Pâques est une fête importante de cette saison. Il y a aussi «la fête des Mères». Cette saison est _____

_____.

les oiseaux *the birds*
les arbres *the trees*
  les gens *people*   portent *wear*
vêtements *clothes*
  Pâques *Easter*
  la fête *the holiday*

2. Cette saison est la favorite de beaucoup d'enfants parce qu'il y a les grandes vacances et il n'y a pas de classes. Il fait très chaud et il fait du soleil. Les enfants vont à la plage pour nager. Les jours sont longs et les nuits sont courtes. Les fêtes importantes sont: «le jour de l'Indépendance» et «la fête des Pères». Cette saison est _____.

les nuits *the nights*   courtes *short*

3. Pendant cette saison les enfants sont tristes parce que les écoles sont ouvertes et c'est la rentrée des classes. Mais c'est une saison agréable. Il ne fait ni très froid ni très chaud. Il fait beau. Il y a beaucoup de fêtes: « la fête du Travail », «le jour de la Découverte de l'Amérique» par Christophe Colomb, «la Toussaint» et «le jour d'Action de grâce». Cette saison est _____.

pendant *during*
ouvertes *open*
la rentrée *the return*
ni . . . ni *neither . . . nor*

la découverte *the discovery*
la Toussaint *All Saint's Day*
grâce *thanks*

4. Aimez-vous le froid? Pendant cette saison il neige et il fait très froid. Les gens portent beaucoup de vêtements pour se protéger. Les nuits sont longues et il y a beaucoup de gens qui trouvent que c'est une saison triste. Pourtant il y a beaucoup de fêtes populaires. Il y a Noël, «Le jour de l'An», «l'anniversaire de George Washington», «l'anniversaire d'Abraham Lincoln» et «la Saint-Valentin».

Cette saison est _____.

se protéger *to protect oneself*

pourtant *still*
Noël *Christmas*

CONVERSATION

VOCABULAIRE

la chaleur *the heat*
affreuse *awful*
la plage *the beach*
pendant *during*
je ne sais pas *I don't know how*
nager *to swim*

DIALOGUE

You are the second person in the dialog. Respond in complete French sentences:

1. Bonjour. Cette chaleur est affreuse, vous ne trouvez pas?

_____

2. Tenez! Moi aussi.

_____

3. Vous allez à la plage tous les jours pendant l'été?

_____

4. Alors, on va dans l'eau?

_____

QUESTIONS PERSONNELLES

1. Quel temps fait-il aujourd'hui?

_____

2. En quelle saison faites-vous des pique-niques?

_____

3. À quelle heure faites-vous vos devoirs?

_____

4. Que faites-vous quand il fait chaud?

_____

5. Que faites-vous en hiver?

_____

VOUS

Pick your favorite season and write a five-sentence composition about it using the following cues:

1. the season you like
2. the weather during your season
3. the holidays during your season
4. two things you do during the season

_____

_____

_____

_____

_____

Révision V (Leçons 17-20)

Leçon 17

40 quarante
50 cinquante
60 soixante
70 soixante-dix
71 soixante et onze
72 soixante-douze
73 soixante-treize
74 soixante-quatorze

75 soixante-quinze
76 soixante-seize
77 soixante-dix-sept

78 soixante-dix-huit

79 soixante-dix-neuf

80 quatre-vingts
81 quatre-vingt-un
82 quatre-vingt-deux

90 quatre-vingt-dix
91 quatre-vingt-onze
92 quatre-vingt-douze
93 quatre-vingt-treize
94 quatre-vingt-quatorze
95 quatre-vingt-quinze
96 quatre-vingt-seize
97 quatre-vingt-dix-sept
98 quatre-vingt-dix-huit
99 quatre-vingt-dix-neuf
100 cent
101 cent un

Leçon 18

Contractions in French:

à + le = au   Use **au** before masculine singular nouns beginning with a consonant.

à + les = aux   Use **aux** before all plural nouns.

Use **à la** before feminine singular nouns beginning with a consonant.

Use **à l'** before masculine and feminine singular nouns beginning with a vowel.

de + le = du   Use **du** before masculine singular nouns beginning with a consonant.

de + les = des   Use **des** before all plural nouns.

Use **de la** before feminine singular nouns beginning with a consonant.

Use **de l'** before masculine and feminine singular nouns beginning with a vowel.

270

Leçon 19

a. The verb **aller** is an irregular verb that means *to go*. All of its forms must be memorized:

je vais	nous allons
tu vas	vous allez
il va	ils vont
elle va	elles vont

The same rules as for **-ER** apply to making a sentence negative or for asking a question.

b. **Aller** is used in expressions of health:

Comment *allez*-vous? *How are you?*
Je *vais* bien. *I am well.*　　　**Je *vais* mal.** *I am not well.*

Leçon 20

a. The verb **faire** is an irregular verb that means *to make, to do*. All of its forms must be memorized:

je fais	nous faisons
tu fais	vous faites
il fait	ils font
elle fait	elles font

The same rules for **-ER** verbs apply when making a sentence negative or asking a question.

b. **Faire** is used in expressions of weather:

Quel temps *fait*-il? *What is the weather?*

Il *fait* froid.	*It's cold.*	**Il *fait* mauvais.**	*It's bad.*
Il *fait* chaud.	*It's warm.*	**Il *fait* du vent.**	*It's windy.*
Il *fait* beau.	*It's beautiful.*	**Il *fait* du soleil.**	*It's sunny.*

Activités

A. Write the French word under the picture you see. Then find the French word in the puzzle:

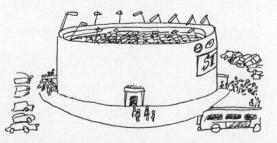　　　

1. _____　　2. _____

3. _____

4. _____

5. _____

6. _____

7. _____

8. _____

9. _____

10. _____

11. _____

12. _____

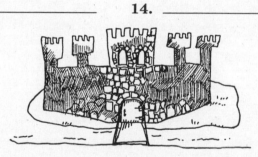

13. _____

14. _____

15. _____

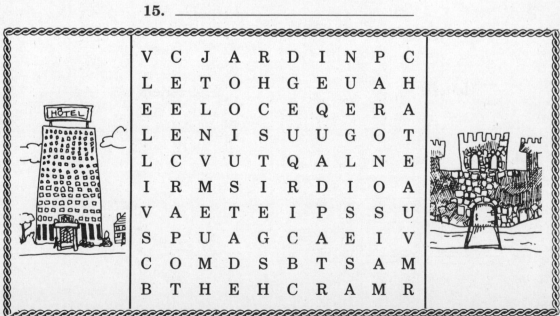

V	C	J	A	R	D	I	N	P	C
L	E	T	O	H	G	E	U	A	H
E	E	L	O	C	E	Q	E	R	A
L	E	N	I	S	U	U	G	O	T
L	C	V	U	T	Q	A	L	N	E
I	R	M	S	I	R	D	I	O	A
V	A	E	T	E	I	P	S	S	U
S	P	U	A	G	C	A	E	I	V
C	O	M	D	S	B	T	S	A	M
B	T	H	E	H	C	R	A	M	R

B. Express the numbers in French and then fit them correctly into the puzzle:

3 letters

6 _____

10 _____

6 letters

4 _____

13 _____

15 _____

30 _____

_____

5 letters

3 _____

12 _____

16 _____

20 _____

4 letters

2 _____

5 _____

7 _____

8 _____

9 _____

11 _____

8 letters

14 _____

40 _____

60 _____

9 letters

50 _____

275

C. Labyrinthe: Every day Pierre leaves his house and walks to his high school, taking the shortest route. On his way he passes many places. Figure out the shortest way to school and list the 15 places he passes:

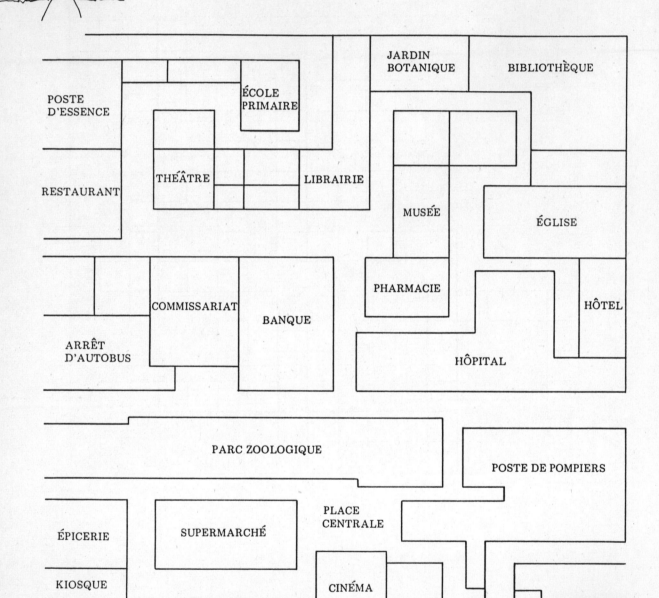

1. _____

2. _____

3. _____

4. _____

5. _____

6. _____

7. _____

8. _____

9. _____

10. _____

11. _____

12. _____

13. _____

14. _____

15. _____

D. Picture Story

Can you read this story? Much of it is in picture form. Whenever you come to a picture, read it as if it were a French word:

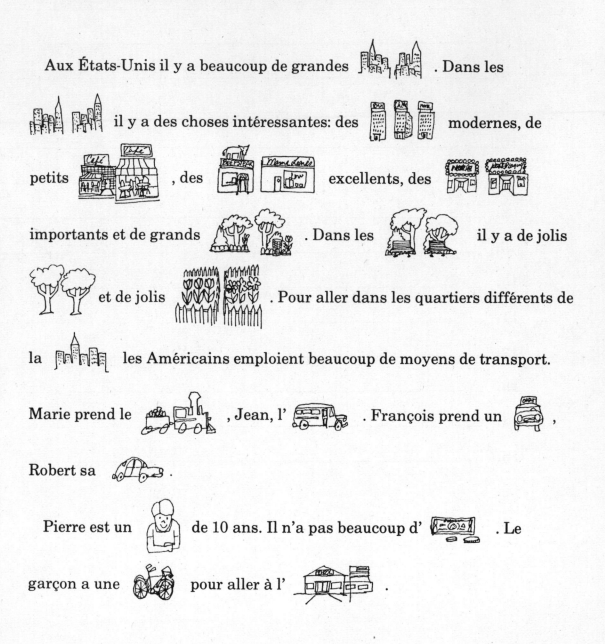

Aux États-Unis il y a beaucoup de grandes [villes]. Dans les

[villes] il y a des choses intéressantes: des [immeubles] modernes, de

petits [cafés], des [restaurants] excellents, des [magasins]

importants et de grands [parcs]. Dans les [parcs] il y a de jolis

[arbres] et de jolis [fleurs]. Pour aller dans les quartiers différents de

la [ville] les Américains emploient beaucoup de moyens de transport.

Marie prend le [train], Jean, l' [autobus]. François prend un [taxi],

Robert sa [voiture].

Pierre est un [garçon] de 10 ans. Il n'a pas beaucoup d' [argent]. Le

garçon a une [bicyclette] pour aller à l' [école].

278

Sixième
Partie

21 | Vouloir et pouvoir

1   Can you guess the meanings of these words?

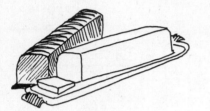

le beurre

le sel

le sucre

le jus

le poulet

le boeuf

le bifteck

le vin

le gâteau

la bouteille

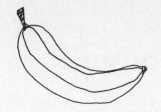

la banane

la cerise

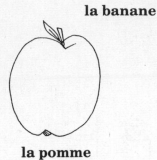

la pomme

la pomme de terre

la carotte

la glace

l'eau

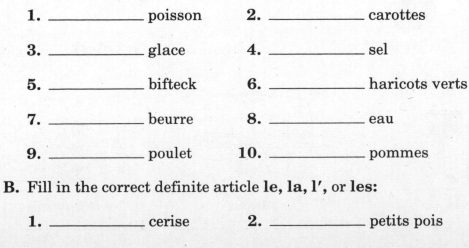

les épinards　　**les haricots verts**　　**les petits pois**

Activités

A. Fill in the correct partitive article **de la, de l', du,** or **des:**

1. _____ poisson
2. _____ carottes
3. _____ glace
4. _____ sel
5. _____ bifteck
6. _____ haricots verts
7. _____ beurre
8. _____ eau
9. _____ poulet
10. _____ pommes

B. Fill in the correct definite article **le, la, l',** or **les:**

1. _____ cerise
2. _____ petits pois

3. _____ banane   **4.** _____ sucre

5. _____ vin   **6.** _____ épinards

7. _____ carotte   **8.** _____ jus

9. _____ gâteau   **10.** _____ beurre

C. Identifiez. Use the correct definite article:

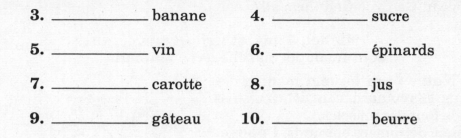

1. _____   **2.** _____

3. _____   **4.** _____   **5.** _____

6. _____   **7.** _____

 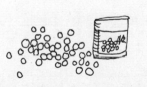 

8. _____   **9.** _____   **10.** _____

2 In the story that follows, all the forms of the irregular verb **vouloir** (*to wish, to want*) appear. Can you find them all?

Michel, 5 ans, et Éric, 8 ans, sont au supermarché avec maman.

MAMAN: **Notre famille veut** manger des épinards. Les épinards sont délicieux. Les épinards font des muscles.

ÉRIC: Moi, je déteste les épinards. **Popeye,** peut-être, **veut** manger des épinards, mais moi, **je veux** manger des haricots verts.

MICHEL: **Tu veux** manger des haricots verts? AÏE! Moi, **je veux** manger des petits pois, s'il te plaît, maman.

MAMAN: **Mes enfants veulent** toujours des légumes différents. Ils ne sont jamais d'accord. Bon. Bon. J'achète des haricots verts et des petits pois. Alors mes enfants, **voulez-vous** du poulet ou du poisson?

ÉRIC: Du poisson, maman!

MICHEL: Du poulet, maman!

MAMAN: Quel désastre! Bon, j'achète du bifteck.

ÉRIC ET MICHEL: Ah non! Pas de bifteck!

MAMAN: Êtes-vous d'accord pour le dessert au moins?

ÉRIC ET MICHEL (après une longue conversation animée): Oui, maman. **Nous voulons** un gâteau au chocolat et de la glace à la vanille.

MAMAN: Enfin!

jamais *never*
d'accord *in agreement*
alors *so*

désastre *disaster*

au moins *at least*

animée *animated*

enfin *finally*

Activité

D. Finissez les phrases:

1. Michel a _____ ans.

2. Éric a _____ ans.

3. Michel, Éric et maman sont au _____ .

4. La famille veut manger _____ parce qu'ils sont délicieux.

5. Éric veut manger _____ .

6. Michel veut manger _____ .

284

7. Comme viande Michel veut _____ .

8. Mais Eric préfère _____ .

9. Alors, maman finit par acheter _____ .

10. Comme dessert les deux garçons veulent _____ .

3 Did you find the forms of the irregular verb **vouloir** in the story? Remember: **vouloir** is a special verb because it is one of a kind. No other verb in French is conjugated exactly like **vouloir**. **Vouloir** means *to wish, to want*. Fill in the proper forms for each subject. MEMORIZE them!

je _____		**nous** _____	
tu _____		**vous** _____	
il _____		**ils** _____	
elle _____		**elles** _____	

4 Good! Now there is another verb in French, **pouvoir** (*to be able to, can*), which resembles **vouloir** when it is conjugated. There are, however, two spelling differences between **pouvoir** and **vouloir**. What are they?

1. _____

2. _____

When you conjugate **pouvoir,** you must make the same changes. See if you can conjugate **pouvoir:**

je _____		**nous** _____	
tu _____		**vous** _____	
il _____		**ils** _____	
elle _____		**elles** _____	

Activités

E. Fill in the correct form of the verb:

1. Je p_____ danser.

2. Nous v_____ chanter.

3. Tu v_____ le livre.

285

4. Vous p_____ écouter le professeur.

5. Il v_____ parler français.

6. Elles v_____ la liste.

7. Marie v_____ le cahier.

8. Paul et Anne p_____ finir.

9. Je v_____ manger.

10. Nous p_____ étudier.

11. Vous v_____ le stylo.

12. Tu p_____ travailler.

F. Make all the sentences in Exercise D negative:

1. _____

2. _____

3. _____

4. _____

5. _____

6. _____

7. _____

8. _____

9. _____

10. _____

11. _____

12. _____

G. Change all the sentences in Exercise D to questions using inversion:

1. _____

2. _____

3. _____

4. _____

5. _____

6. _____

7. _____

8. _____

9. _____

10. _____

11. _____

12. _____

H. Complete the following sentences with a form of **vouloir** and the object shown in each picture:

1. Tu _____ un _____ .

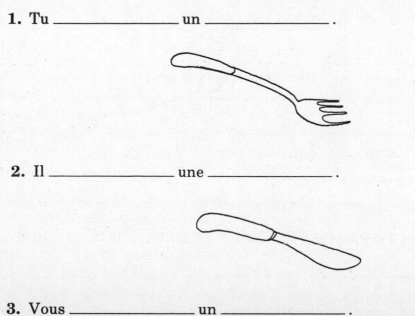

2. Il _____ une _____ .

3. Vous _____ un _____ .

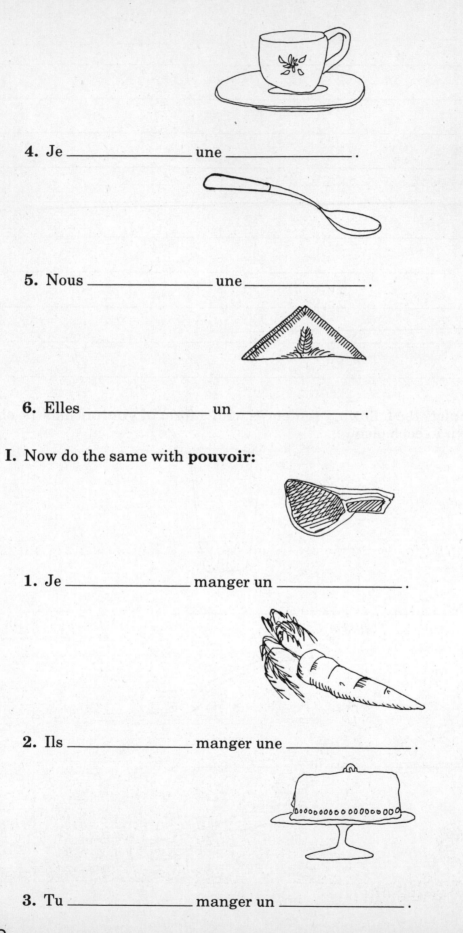

4. Je _____ une _____ .

5. Nous _____ une _____ .

6. Elles _____ un _____ .

I. Now do the same with **pouvoir:**

1. Je _____ manger un _____ .

2. Ils _____ manger une _____ .

3. Tu _____ manger un _____ .

4. Sylvie _____ manger du _____ .

5. Nous _____ manger de la _____ .

6. Vous _____ manger des _____ .

J. Study the following picture. Then see if you can answer the questions about it:

1. Quels fruits est-ce qu'il y a?

   _____

2. À quel rayon est-ce qu'il y a du poulet?

   _____

3. Combien de personnes est-ce qu'il y a au supermarché?

   _____

4. Quels légumes est-ce qu'il y a?

   _____

5. Où sont les œufs?

   _____

6. Quelle sorte de viande est-ce qu'il y a?

   _____

7. Combien de sortes de fruits est-ce qu'il y a?

   _____

8. Combien de boîtes de lait est-ce qu'il y a?

   _____

9. Qu'est-ce qu'il y a dans les bouteilles?

   _____

10. À quel rayon est-ce qu'il y a des tomates?

   _____

QUESTIONS PERSONNELLES

1. Qu'est-ce que vous aimez manger?

   _____

2. Qu'est-ce que vous aimez boire (*drink*)?

   _____

3. Quels légumes voulez-vour pour le dîner ce soir?

_____

4. Quel dessert voulez-vous pour le déjeuner?

_____

5. À quelle heure pouvez-vous faire vos devoirs?

_____

6. À quelle heure votre mère peut-elle préparer le dîner?

_____

7. Pouvez-vous nager?

_____

VOUS

You are a talented and clever person applying for a job. Make a list of all the things you can do and that you want included in your resume. EXAMPLE: **Je peux travailler comme secrétaire.**

1. _____

2. _____

3. _____

4. _____

5. _____

UNE SURPRISE-PARTIE

You are having a catered party. Make a list of all the foods you would (and would not) include on the menu:

Oui

1. _____

2. _____

3. _____

4. _____

5. _____

Non

1. _____

2. _____

3. _____

4. _____

5. _____

1 Can you guess the meanings of these new words?

le chapeau

le manteau

le pantalon

le complet

le pull-over

le sac

le maillot de bain

le veston

la jupe

la blouse

la robe

la chemise

la cravate

la ceinture

les vêtements

les chaussettes

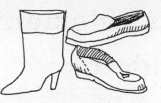
**les chaussures
(les souliers)**

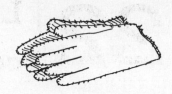
les gants

Activités

A. Robert has just gotten a job in a clothing store. The boss asks him to pin labels on the models so that the prices can be put on later. Can you help him?

LABELS

la chemise   la jupe   le manteau
les chaussures   la blouse   le chapeau
le veston   la robe   le pull-over
le pantalon   les gants   la ceinture
la cravate   le complet

B. Write the French article of clothing for the English meanings:

1. the bathing suit _____

2. the dress _____

3. the overcoat _____

4. the blouse _____

5. the suit _____

6. the pants _____

7. the socks _____

8. the belt _____

9. the skirt _____

10. the shirt _____

11. the tie _____

12. the hat _____

13. the gloves _____

14. the pocketbook _____

2 Now read this story and see if you can answer the questions about it:

RENÉE: Maman, regarde cette invitation à l'anniversaire de Thérèse. Maintenant j'ai besoin de nouveaux vêtements.

l'anniversaire *the birthday*
j'ai besoin de *I need*
nouveaux *new*

MAMAN: Mais ma chérie, tu as de très jolis vêtements.

RENÉE: Non, maman. Mes vêtements sont vieux. Et c'est une fête importante. Tous les garçons vont être là, surtout Gérard.

vieux *old*
là *there*   **surtout** *especially*

MAMAN: D'accord. Demain nous allons acheter quelque chose au grand magasin.

quelque chose *something*

Dans le grand magasin.

LA VENDEUSE: Bonjour. Vous désirez?

MAMAN: Ma fille va aller à une fête samedi soir et nous voulons acheter de nouveaux vêtements pour elle.

RENÉE: Des vêtements à la dernière mode.

à la dernière mode *in the latest style*

LA VENDEUSE: Bien sûr. Que pensez-vous de cette mini-jupe avec cette blouse bleue?

RENÉE: C'est parfait. Et regarde aussi cette paire de chaussures, cette ceinture et ce chapeau.

MAMAN: Tu vas être la fille la plus chic de la fête.

Plus tard, chez elle, Renée parle au téléphone avec Thérèse.

plus tard *later*

THÉRÈSE: Cette fête va être sensationnelle. Tout le monde va venir habillé d'une façon ridicule.

habillé *dressed*
d'une façon *in a manner*

RENÉE: Oh mon Dieu!

Activité

C. Répondez aux questions:

1. Qu'est-ce que Renée et la maman regardent?

   _____

2. Qu'est-ce que Renée veut acheter?

   _____

3. Pourquoi est-ce que cette fête est importante?

   _____

4. Où est-ce que Renée achète ses vêtements?

   _____

5. Quand est-ce que Renée va aller à la fête?

   _____

6. Quelle sorte de vêtements veut-elle porter?

   _____

7. De quelle couleur est la blouse?

   _____

8. Avec qui Renée parle-t-elle au téléphone?

   _____

9. Comment tout le monde va-t-il venir à la surprise-partie?

   _____

10. Renée est-elle contente maintenant?

    _____

3 Learn the names of the colors:

rouge (*red*)	**gris** (*gray*)	**blanc** (*white*)
jaune (*yellow*)	**vert** (*green*)	**mauve** (*purple*)
orange	**brun** (*brown*)	**noir** (*black*)
rose	**bleu**	

4 Now look at these phrases:

I	II
un pantalon *bleu*	une robe *bleue*
un pantalon *noir*	une robe *noire*

In Group I, what is the gender of **pantalon?** _____

In Group II, what is the gender of **robe?** _____

How is the adjective describing the feminine noun different from the adjective

describing the masculine noun? _____

What is the position of the adjective with respect to the noun? _____

_____

Repeat the phrases in both Groups after your teacher. Do the masculine and

feminine adjective sound the same or different? _____

5

un pantalon *gris*	une robe *grise*
un pantalon *vert*	une robe *verte*
un pantalon *brun*	une robe *brune*
un pantalon *blanc*	une robe *blanche*

How is the adjective describing the feminine noun different from the adjective

describing the masculine noun? _____

What is the position of the adjective with respect to the noun? _____

_____

Repeat the phrases in both groups after your teacher. Do the masculine and

feminine adjectives sound the same or different? _____

What special spelling change is there for the adjective **blanc** in the feminine?

_____

6

un pantalon *rouge*	une robe *rouge*
un pantalon *jaune*	une robe *jaune*
un pantalon *orange*	une robe *orange*
un pantalon *rose*	une robe *rose*
un pantalon *mauve*	une robe *mauve*

Is the adjective describing the feminine noun different from the adjective describing the masculine noun? _____

Why didn't we have to make any changes for the feminine form? _____

_____

What is the position of the adjective with respect to the noun? _____

_____

Repeat the phrases in both groups after your teacher. Do the masculine and feminine adjectives sound the same or different? _____

7 What letter do you add to **pantalon** and **robe** to make them plural? _____

What letter do you add to the name of the color to make it plural? _____

Why wouldn't you add **s** to **gris?** _____

Activités

D. Identify the object and the color. Use the correct indefinite article. Follow the example:

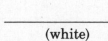

1. __**une jupe bleue**__
   (blue)

2. _____
   (white)

3. _____
   (gray)

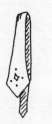

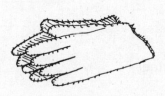

4. _____
   (purple)

5. _____
   (green)

6. _____
   (brown)

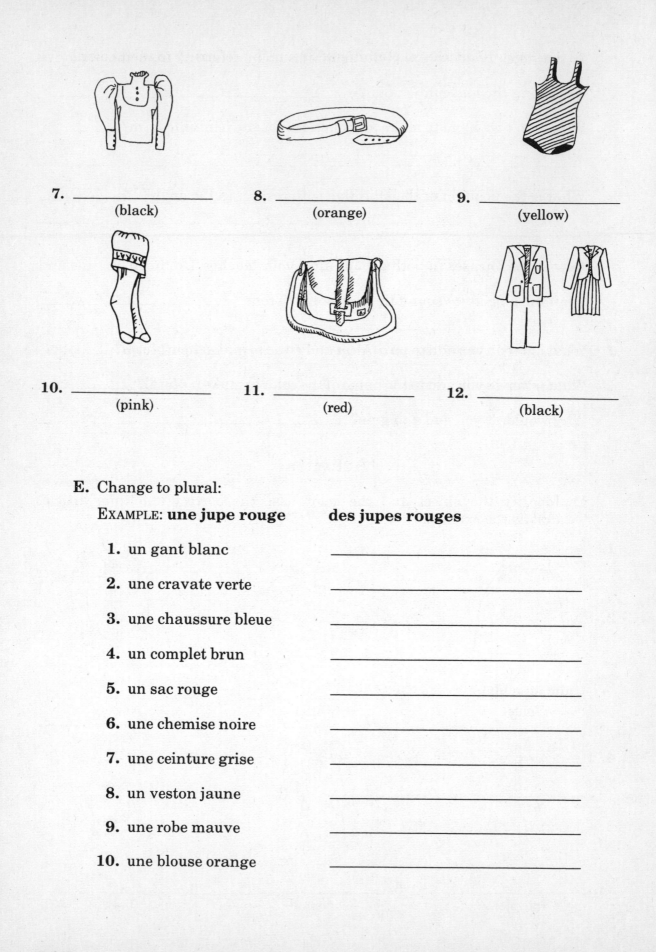

7. _____
(black)

8. _____
(orange)

9. _____
(yellow)

10. _____
(pink)

11. _____
(red)

12. _____
(black)

E. Change to plural:

EXAMPLE: **une jupe rouge**   **des jupes rouges**

1. un gant blanc _____

2. une cravate verte _____

3. une chaussure bleue _____

4. un complet brun _____

5. un sac rouge _____

6. une chemise noire _____

7. une ceinture grise _____

8. un veston jaune _____

9. une robe mauve _____

10. une blouse orange _____

F. Describe 10 articles of clothing in French by referring to their color:

EXAMPLE: **La robe est *noire*.**

1. _____

2. _____

3. _____

4. _____

5. _____

6. _____

7. _____

8. _____

9. _____

10. _____

QUESTIONS PERSONNELLES

1. Que portez-vous quand il fait froid?

_____

2. En quelle saison portez-vous un maillot de bain?

_____

3. De quelle couleur est votre pantalon?

_____

4. De quelle couleur est votre chemise?

_____

5. Où portez-vous des gants?

_____

299

CONVERSATION

VOCABULAIRE

tard *late*
le lit *the bed*
à côté de *beside*

mon chéri *my darling*
sur *on*

sous *under*
mon amour *my love*

DIALOGUE

You are the second person in the dialog. Answer the questions in French:

Mon Dieu, Alice. Il est tard. Où est ma chemise?

_____

Ma cravate bleue. Où est ma cravate bleue?

_____

Maintenant. Où sont mes souliers? Où sont-ils Alice?

_____

Alice, où est mon chapeau?

_____

VOUS

You have been given money to celebrate a special holiday or occasion. You decide to buy 5 articles of clothing that you love. Describe them, now that they are yours:

EXAMPLE: **mon chapeau bleu**

1. _____   2. _____

3. _____   4. _____

5. _____

23 | Les animaux

1 Can you guess the meanings of these words?

le chien

le chat

le cochon

le cheval

le lion

le tigre

le loup

le renard

le lapin

le mouton

le singe

l'éléphant (*m.*)

l'âne (*m.*)

l'oiseau (*m.*)

la poule

la vache

la chèvre

Activités

A. Identifiez. Use the correct definite article:

1. _____   2. _____

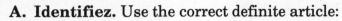

3. _____   4. _____   5. _____

6. _____   7. _____

8. _____   9. _____   10. _____

B. Put the animals in groups:

Animaux domestiques	Animaux de la ferme	Animaux sauvages
_____	_____	_____
_____	_____	_____
	_____	_____
	_____	_____
	_____	_____
	_____	_____
	_____	_____
	_____	

C. Qui suis-je? Now that we know the French names of some animals, let's see if we can figure out who they are by their descriptions:

1. Je suis un animal de la ferme. Je mange de l'herbe. Je suis grand et intelligent. Je transporte les gens et les objets. J'aide avec le travail. Je

   cours rapidement. Je suis _____

   _____.

   la ferme *the farm*
   l'herbe *the grass*
   gens *people*
   le travail *the work*
   cours *run*

2. Je suis très petit. Je mange de la viande. Mon père est le meilleur ami des hommes. Je n'aime pas les

   chats. Je suis _____.

   le meilleur *the best*

3. Je suis grande et stupide. J'habite la campagne. Je mange de l'herbe toute la journée. Je donne du lait.

Je suis _____.

4. Je suis un animal sauvage. Je suis comme un chien. Je mange de la viande. Quand les gens me voient,

ils courent. Je suis _____

_____.

voient *see*
courent *run*

5. Je suis l'animal le plus grand de la terre. Je ne suis pas féroce. Je mange de l'herbe. J'ai un très grand nez que j'emploie comme une main.

Je suis _____.

6. J'habite les maisons des gens. J'habite aussi les rues. Je n'aime pas les chiens. Je mange les souris.

Je suis _____.

les souris *the mice*

7. J'habite la campagne. Je suis une sorte d'oiseau. Je donne des œufs.

Je mange du maïs. Je suis _____

_____.

8. Je suis un animal très gros. Tout le monde dit que je suis très sale. On fait de moi du porc, du jambon et beaucoup d'autres choses. Je suis

_____.

gros *fat*
tout le monde *everybody*

9. Je suis un animal très intelligent. J'habite les arbres. J'aide les gens avec leurs recherches. Je suis aussi dans les jardins zoologiques et les

cirques. Je suis _____

_____.

les arbres *the trees*
la recherche *the research*
le cirque *the circus*

10. Je suis un animal de la campagne. De ma laine on fait des manteaux, des pull-overs et d'autres vête-

la campagne *the country*
la laine *the wool*

ments. Je suis _____

_____ .

D. Match the foods with the animals they come from. Write the number and matching letter in the space provided:

1. les œufs
2. le poulet
3. la glace
4. le jambon
5. le fromage
6. le lait
7. le porc
8. le hamburger
9. le beurre
10. le bifteck

a. le cochon   _____

b. la vache   _____

c. la poule   _____

E. Can you name all the animals on Pierre's farm? Start each sentence with **Je vois** (*I see*):

1. _____   2. _____

3. _____   4. _____

5. _____   6. _____

7. _____   8. _____

306

F. Find the hidden animals. There are 10 animals hidden in this picture. Find them and list them below:

_____

_____

_____

_____

_____

2 In the story that follows, all the forms of the irregular verb **voir** (*to see*) appear. See if you can find them all:

Je m'appelle Georges. J'ai un petit appartement. De ma fenêtre **je vois** des gens qui passent. **Les gens** me **voient** aussi. Ils pensent que je suis drôle. Un jour, un jeune garçon arrive chez moi. **Il** me **voit.** Il me **regarde** pendant une demi-heure. Il me demande: «Est-ce que **tu** me **vois?**» Mais je ne réponds pas. Ce gentil garçon me donne une banane à manger. J'adore les bananes. Mon ami et moi, quand **nous voyons** des gens avec des bananes, nous sommes très excités et nous sautons partout. Quand je finis la banane je suis très content et je jette une cacahouète au garçon pour dire «merci». Le garçon est très surpris. Pourquoi? Mais parce que, **voyez-vous,** je suis un singe.

drôle *funny*

pendant *for*
me *me*
gentil *nice*

sautons *jump*
　partout *everywhere*
　jette *throw*
une cacahouète *a peanut*

Activité

G. Répondez aux questions:

1. Quel est le nom du narrateur?

_____

2. Que voit-il de sa fenêtre?

_____

3. Qu'est-ce que les gens pensent de Georges?

_____

4. Comment est l'appartement de Georges?

_____

5. Qui arrive un jour?

_____

6. Qu'est-ce qu'il donne à Georges?

_____

7. Que font Georges et son ami quand ils voient des bananes?

   _____

8. Que jette-t-il au garçon?

   _____

9. Comment est le garçon?

   _____

10. Qui est Georges?

   _____

3 Did you find the forms of the irregular verb **voir** in the story? Remember: **voir** is a special verb because it is one of a kind. No other verb in French is conjugated exactly like **voir. Voir** means *to see*. Fill in the proper forms for each subject. MEMORIZE them!

je _____   nous _____

tu _____   vous _____

il _____   ils _____

elle _____   elles _____

H. Fill in the correct form of the verb **voir:**

1. Nous _____ le taxi.

2. Je _____ la voiture rouge.

3. Paul _____ bien.

4. Vous _____ l'hôtel.

5. Elles _____ le tableau.

6. Tu _____ mon chat.

7. Il _____ la maison.

8. Ma grand-mère _____ le livre.

9. Ils _____ le film.

10. Elle _____ l'école.

I. Make all the sentences in Exercise H negative:

1. _____

2. _____

3. _____

4. _____

5. _____

6. _____

7. _____

8. _____

9. _____

10. _____

J. Change all the sentences in Exercise H to questions using inversion:

1. _____

2. _____

3. _____

4. _____

5. _____

6. _____

7. _____

8. _____

9. _____

10. _____

CONVERSATION

André, veux-tu habiter avec moi en ville?

Je ne sais pas, Richard. J'aime beaucoup la campagne.

En ville il y a beaucoup de gens et beaucoup à faire.

Je sais. Mais tous mes amis sont ici.

Ça n'a pas d'importance. Il y a plus de garçons en ville.

Je ne peux pas vivre sans mes amis Caramel et Cyclone.

Mon ami, qui sont Caramel et Cyclone?

Cyclone est mon cheval et Caramel est mon chien.

VOCABULAIRE

en ville *in town*　　　**la campagne** *the country(side)*　　　**plus de** *more than*

DIALOGUE

Fill in the words that are missing in the dialog. Choose from the list provided below:

André, veux-tu _____ avec moi en _____?

     Je ne sais pas, Richard. J'aime beaucoup _____.

En ville il y a beaucoup de _____ et beaucoup à _____.

     Je sais, mais tous mes _____ sont ici.

Ça n'a pas _____. Il y a plus de _____ en ville.

     Je ne peux pas _____ sans mes amis Caramel et Cyclone.

Mon ami, _____ sont Caramel et Cyclone?

     Cyclone est mon _____ et Caramel est mon _____.

ville	habiter	gens
faire	garçons	qui
cheval	la campagne	amis
d'importance	chien	vivre

QUESTIONS PERSONNELLES

1. Quel est votre animal favori?

_____

2. Quel animal est-ce que vous n'aimez pas?

_____

3. Quel animal est stupide?

_____

4. Quel animal est intelligent?

_____

5. Quel animal donne du lait?

_____

VOUS

Name the animals you see when you take a trip to the zoo:

1. Je vois _____

2. _____

3. _____

4. _____

5. _____

24 | Je suis américain. Je suis américaine.

1

PAYS	NATIONALITÉ	LANGUE
les États-Unis *m. pl.*	américain(e)	anglais
l'Angleterre *f.*	anglais(e)	anglais
le Canada	canadien(ne)	français, anglais
l'Espagne *f.*	espagnol(e)	espagnol
la France	français(e)	français
l'Haïti *f.*	haïtien(ne)	français, créole
l'Italie *f.*	italien(ne)	italien
l'Allemagne *f.*	allemand(e)	allemand
la Russie	russe	russe
la Chine	chinois(e)	chinois
le Japon	japonais(e)	japonais

Activités

A. For each name, give the nationality of the person and the country he or she comes from:

1. Pablo _____

2. Mario _____

3. François _____

4. Mary _____

5. Natasha _____

6. Hans _____

7. Han-Ling _____

8. Marie-Hélène _____

B. Match the dish with the country it comes from. Write the number and matching letter in the space provided:

1. pizza   **a.** la Russie   _____

2. borscht   **b.** le Japon   _____

314

3. sukiyaki   **c.** l'Angleterre _____

4. wonton soup   **d.** l'Haïti _____

5. crêpes suzette   **e.** l'Italie _____

6. paella   **f.** la France _____

7. beef and kidney pie **g.** la Chine _____

8. riz créole   **h.** l'Espagne _____

2 Now look carefully at the following sentences:

I	II

J'aime *la France*   **Je vais aller** *en France.*
J'aime *la Chine.*   **Je vais voyager** *en Chine.*
J'aime *la Russie.* **Je vais travailler** *en Russie.*

In Group I, what is the gender of the names of the countries? _____

How do you know? _____

In Group II, what word is used to say "TO or IN the country"? _____

3 Now compare these sentences:

I	II

J'aime *le Canada.*   **Je vais aller** *au Canada.*
J'aime *le Japon.*   **Je vais voyager** *au Japon.*

In Group I, what is the gender of the names of the countries? _____

How do you know? _____

In Group II, what word is used to say "TO or IN the country"? _____

4   I   II

J'aime *les États-Unis.*   **Je vais travailler** *aux États-Unis.*

In Group I, what is the gender of the United States? _____

How do you know? _____

Is the United States a singular or plural noun? _____

How do you know? _____

In Group II, what word is used to say "TO or IN the United States"? _____

5 Summary

To say TO or IN a specific country, use

en before _____

au before _____

aux before _____

6 Compare these sentences:

J'aime _la France_.	Je suis _français_.	Je suis _de la France_.
J'aime _l'Italie_.	Je suis _italien_.	Je suis _de l'Italie_.
J'aime _le Canada_.	Je suis _canadien_.	Je suis _du Canada_.
J'aime _les États-Unis_.	Je suis _américain_.	Je suis _des États-Unis_.

What is the meaning of **de la, de l', du,** and **des** in these sentences? _____

_____

When do you use **de la, de l',** **du,** or **des**?

Use **de la** before _____

Use **de l'** before _____

Use **du** before _____

Use **des** before _____

Activités

C. Complete the sentences with **en, au,** or **aux** before the name of the country:

1. Je vais _____ Japon.

2. Nous travaillons _____ Allemagne.

3. Vous êtes _____ Espagne.

4. Elle voyage _____ États-Unis.

5. Tu arrives _____ France.

6. Ils vont _____ Angleterre.

7. Il travaille _____ Canada.

8. Je suis _____ Haïti.

316

9. Vous voyagez _____ Chine.

10. Il arrive _____ Italie.

D. Complete the sentences with **du, de la, de l'**, or **des** before the name of the country:

1. Je suis _____ États-Unis.

2. Il est _____ Russie.

3. Nous sommes _____ Italie.

4. Vous êtes _____ France.

5. Tu es _____ Espagne.

6. Ils sont _____ Angleterre.

7. Elle est _____ Chine.

8. Elles sont _____ Japon.

9. Vous êtes _____ Canada.

10. Tu es _____ Allemagne.

7 Read the following passage and see if you can answer the questions about it:

Dans le monde il y a beaucoup de pays et beaucoup de langues. Savez-vous qu'il y a plus de mille langues dans le monde aujourd'hui? Généralement chaque pays a sa langue officielle. En France, c'est le français; en Espagne, c'est l'espagnol; en Italie, c'est l'italien; en Allemagne, c'est l'allemand. Mais certains pays ont au moins deux langues officielles. En Suisse, par exemple, on parle français, allemand et italien. Au Canada les deux langues officielles sont le français et l'anglais. Dans la Nouvelle-Orléans, le français est une langue semi-officielle. Il y a des journaux, des magazines, des films, des programmes de radio et de télévision tout en français. Il y a beaucoup de personnes qui parlent français dans leur vie quotidienne. Le français est aussi une langue internationale. On parle français à la Martinique, en Haïti, en Afrique et partout dans le monde.

le monde *the world*
  pays *countries*
  savez-vous *do you know*
  mille *1000*
chaque *each*

au moins *at least*

tout *all*

vie quotidienne *daily life*

317

Aux Nations unies il y a six langues officielles. Savez-vous quelles six langues? Voici une liste de langues. Choisissez les six langues officielles:

les Nations unies *the United Nations*

l'allemand   le japonais
l'espagnol   le chinois
l'arabe   l'anglais
le français   l'italien
le russe

La réponse: Les six langues officielles des Nations unies sont: le français, l'anglais, le russe, le chinois, l'arabe et l'espagnol.

la réponse *the answer*

Et maintenant, voyez-vous pourquoi la langue française est si importante pour vous?

si *so*

Activités

E. Répondez aux questions:

1. Combien de langues y a-t-il dans le monde?

_____

2. Généralement, combien de langues officielles a chaque pays?

_____

3. Quelles sont les langues officielles de la Suisse?

_____

4. Quelles sont les langues officielles du Canada?

_____

5. Quelle langue parlez-vous?

_____

6. Où y a-t-il des programmes de radio et de télévision en français?

_____

7. Où parle-t-on français?

_____

8. Combien de langues officielles y a-t-il aux Nations unies?

_____

9. Quelles sont ces langues officielles?

_____

10. Pourquoi la langue française est-elle importante?

_____

F. Fill in the correct information:

1. Nous sommes aux _____,

où habitent les _____.

Ils parlent _____.

2. Nous sommes en _____,

où habitent les _____.

Ils parlent _____.

3. Nous sommes en _____,

où habitent les _____.

Ils parlent _____.

4. Nous sommes en _____,

où habitent les _____.

Ils parlent _____.

5. Nous sommes en _____,

où habitent les _____.

Ils parlent _____.

6. Nous sommes en _____,

où habitent les _____.

Ils parlent _____.

7. Nous sommes en _____,

où habitent les _____.

Ils parlent _____.

8. Nous sommes en _____,

où habitent les _____.

Ils parlent _____.

8 Look at the following sentences carefully:

André est *allemand*.	Sylvie est *allemande*.
François est *français*.	Françoise est *française*.
Jean est *américain*.	Jeanne est *américaine*.
Marc est *anglais*.	Anne est *anglaise*.
Paul est *japonais*.	Marie est *japonaise*.
Luc est *chinois*.	Régine est *chinoise*.
Raoul est *espagnol*.	Marie est *espagnole*.
Ivan est *russe*.	Olga est *russe*.

How are the feminine adjectives different from the masculine adjectives?

_____

Repeat the sentences after your teacher. How is the sound different for the

feminine adjectives? _____

Which adjectives do NOT have a sound change? _____

320

Which is the only adjective that does NOT have a spelling change? _____

Why? _____

Using the rules you have learned in the past, how would you make the

adjectives plural? _____

Ils sont allemand_____   Elles sont allemande_____

Ils sont américain_____   Elles sont américaine_____

Ils sont espagnol_____   Elles sont espagnole_____

Ils sont anglais_____   Elles sont anglaise_____

Ils sont français_____   Elles sont française_____

Ils sont japonais_____   Elles sont japonaise_____

Ils sont chinois_____   Elles sont chinoise_____

Ils sont russe _____   Elles sont russe_____

Activité

G. Fill in the correct form of the adjective:

    1. (anglais)   Anne est _____.

    2. (russe)   Raoul est _____.

    3. (espagnol)   Les filles sont _____.

    4. (chinois)   Les garçons sont _____.

    5. (américain)   Ils sont _____.

    6. (français)   Marie est _____.

    7. (japonais)   Suzanne et Sylvie sont _____.

    8. (allemand)   Elles sont _____.

9 Now look at these sentences:

    Jean-Pierre est haïtien.   **Marie-Hélène est *haïtienne*.**
    Mario est italien.   **Marie est *italienne*.**
    Jean est canadien.   **Jeanne est *canadienne*.**

If a masculine adjective ends in **-ien,** how do you form the feminine of the adjective? _____

How would you form the masculine plural? feminine plural? _____

Complete these sentences:

Jean-Pierre et Henri sont haïtien_____.

Marie-Hélène et Carine sont haïtienne_____.

Mario et Giuseppe sont italien_____.

Marie et Carmen sont italienne_____.

Jean et Marc sont canadien_____.

Jeanne et Sylvie sont canadienne_____.

NOTE: When speaking about the nationality of a person, is the name of the nationality in French written with capital or small letter? _____

Activité

H. Fill in the correct form of the adjective:

1. (haïtien)   Les garçons sont _____.

2. (italien)   Mario est _____.

3. (canadien)   Claude est _____.

4. (haïtien)   Sylvie est _____.

5. (italien)   Les grands-pères sont _____.

6. (canadien)   Anne est _____.

7. (haïtien)   Les jeunes filles sont _____.

8. (italien)   Marie est _____.

9. (canadien)   Les mères sont _____.

10. (haïtien)   Pierre est _____.

322

CONVERSATION

Comment s'appelle l'organisation de tous les pays?

C'est facile. Elle s'appelle les Nations unies.

Très bien. Quelles sont les langues officielles de cette organisation?

Le français, l'anglais, l'espagnol, le russe, l'arabe et le chinois.

Magnifique. Où est l'édifice central des Nations unies?

Il est dans la première avenue à New York.

Mais vous êtes très intelligent.

C'est vrai. Mon père est ambassadeur.

VOCABULAIRE

le pays *the country*   **l'édifice** *the building*
facile *easy*   **ambassadeur** (m.) *ambassador*

DIALOGUE

You are the first person in the dialog. Ask the questions that correspond to the answers:

_____

    Elle s'appelle les Nations unies.

_____

    L'anglais, l'arabe, le chinois, l'espagnol, le français et le russe.

_____

    Il est à New York.

_____

    C'est vrai. Ma mère est professeur.

QUESTIONS PERSONNELLES

1. Quelles langues parlez-vous?

_____

2. Quelle est votre nationalité?

_____

3. D'où êtes-vous?

_____

VOUS

You have just won a trip to go anywhere in the world. List in order of your preference the countries you would most like to visit and what language is spoken there:

EXAMPLE: **Je voudrais visiter la France. On parle français en France.**

1. _____

2. _____

3. _____

4. _____

5. _____

Révision VI (Leçons 21-24)

Leçon 21

The verbs **vouloir** (*to wish, to want*) and **pouvoir** (*to be able to, can*) are irregular verbs. All of their forms must be memorized:

vouloir	pouvoir
je veux	je peux
tu veux	tu peux
il veut	il peut
elle veut	elle peut
nous voulons	nous pouvons
vous voulez	vous pouvez
ils veulent	ils peuvent
elles veulent	elles peuvent

The same rules as for **-ER** verbs apply for making a sentence negative or for asking a question.

Leçon 22

a. Adjectives agree in number and gender with the nouns they modify.

b. To get the feminine form of an adjective, add **e** to the masculine form. If the masculine form already ends in **e**, add nothing to form the feminine. If an adjective already ends in **s**, add nothing to form the plural.

c. Adjectives usually follow the nouns they modify.

Leçon 23

The verb **voir** is an irregular verb that means *to see*. All of its forms must be memorized:

je vois	nous voyons
tu vois	vous voyez
il voit	ils voient
elle voit	elles voient

The same rules as for **-ER** verbs apply when making a sentence negative or asking a question.

Leçon 24

If a masculine adjective ends in **ien,** the feminine form of the adjective ends in **ienne.** Add **s** to form the plural of the masculine or feminine form of the adjective.

Activités

A. Write the French word under the picture you see. Then find the French word in the puzzle:

1. _____ 2. _____ 3. _____

4. _____ 5. _____ 6. _____

7. _____ 8. _____ 9. _____

10. _____ 11. _____ 12. _____

```
E  S  T  N  A  G  U  S  O  P
T  I  E  G  N  A  A  U  M  J
A  E  S  S  E  C  A  S  U  N
V  V  S  P  I  O  L  P  T  O
A  R  A  U  N  M  E  A  P  L
R  H  U  O  O  P  E  C  C  A
C  A  E  U  T  L  T  H  H  T
B  L  B  T  S  E  B  O  C  N
O  U  O  L  E  T  S  A  R  A
S  R  R  E  V  O  L  L  U  P
```

326

B. Jumbles: Unscramble the words. Then unscramble the letters in the circles to find out the message:

I

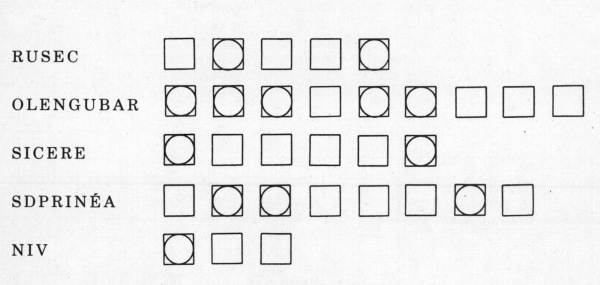

RUSEC

OLENGUBAR

SICERE

SDPRINÉA

NIV

Ce qu'un Français boit (*drinks*) **quand il a très soif:** _____

II

MOMEP

EAGLC

NEVIDA

SPONOIS

SBLTEIUEOL

Pourquoi Paul est populaire: _____

C. Place the names of these animals correctly in the puzzle:

3 LETTERS	4 LETTERS	5 LETTERS	6 LETTERS
âne	lion	tigre	chèvre
	chat	vache	cheval
	loup	chien	mouton
		singe	cochon
		poule	oiseau
		lapin	renard
			souris

D. Jean is an export manager at LaTour & Cie. He is sending out catalogs to several important customers. The company puts out its catalogs in different languages. Help Jean send out the right one:

LATOUR & CIE.

Exportation de vins français

	CLIENT	PAYS	LANGUE
1.	Helmut Kraus	Allemagne	_____
2.	François La Mer	France	_____
3.	Rick Jackson	États-Unis	_____
4.	Antonia Bollavolunta	Italie	_____
5.	Marco Perez	Espagne	_____
6.	Magalie Joseph	Haïti	_____
7.	David Cantrell	Angleterre	_____
8.	Ronald Fong	Chine	_____
9.	Janine Dupont	Montréal, Canada	_____
10.	Léopold M'Boto	Sénégal	_____

E. Picture Story

Can you read this story? Much of it is in picture form. Whenever you come to a picture, read it as if it were a French word:

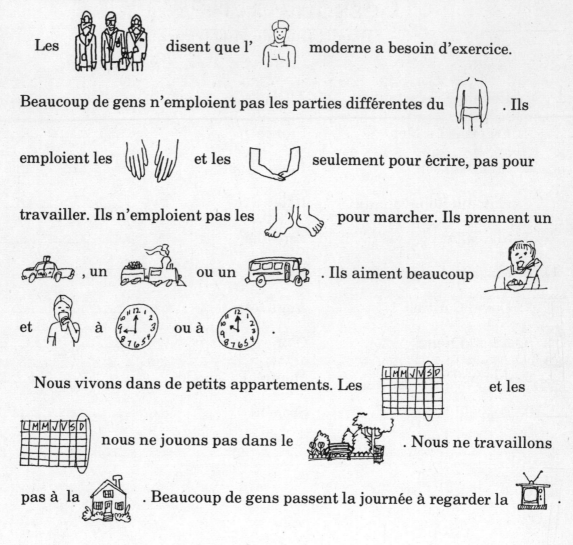

Les disent que l' moderne a besoin d'exercice.

Beaucoup de gens n'emploient pas les parties différentes du . Ils

emploient les et les seulement pour écrire, pas pour

travailler. Ils n'emploient pas les pour marcher. Ils prennent un

, un ou un . Ils aiment beaucoup

et à ou à .

Nous vivons dans de petits appartements. Les et les

nous ne jouons pas dans le . Nous ne travaillons

pas à la . Beaucoup de gens passent la journée à regarder la .

VOCABULAIRE

écrire *write* **la journée** *the day*
prennent *take*

Achievement Test II
(Lessons 13-24)

1 Vocabulary [15 points]

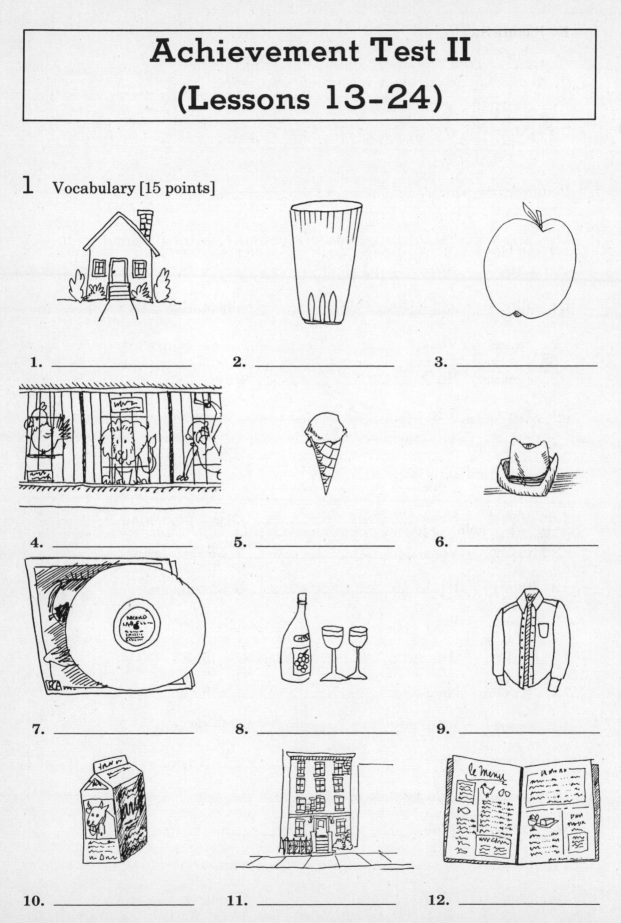

1. _____

2. _____

3. _____

4. _____

5. _____

6. _____

7. _____

8. _____

9. _____

10. _____

11. _____

12. _____

13. _____   14. _____   15. _____

2 Irregular Verbs: **aller, faire, vouloir, pouvoir, voir** [20 points]

Fill in the correct form of the verb:

1. (aller)   Je _____ à la classe.

2. (faire)   Vous _____ les devoirs.

3. (vouloir) Il _____ le livre.

4. (voir)   Elle _____ le garçon.

5. (pouvoir) Je _____ chanter.

6. (aller)   Elles _____ à l'école.

7. (faire)   Nous _____ une promenade.

8. (aller)   Vous _____ au restaurant.

9. (voir)   Ils _____ le monument.

10. (pouvoir) Vous _____ danser.

11. (aller)   Il _____ au cirque.

12. (vouloir) Nous _____ aller au cinéma.

13. (voir)   Vous _____ le tableau.

14. (faire)   Elles _____ le travail.

15. (faire)   Qu'est-ce que tu _____?

16. (aller)   Paul _____ au théâtre.

17. (faire)   Je _____ tout.

18. (vouloir) Elles _____ entrer.

19. (pouvoir) Ils _____ visiter la France.

20. (voir) Je _____ bien.

3 **Quelle heure est-il?** Telling time [10 points]

1. Il est _____

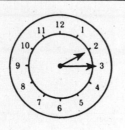

2. Il est _____ et _____

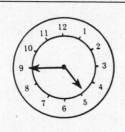

3. Il est _____ et _____

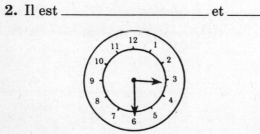

4. Il est _____ moins le _____

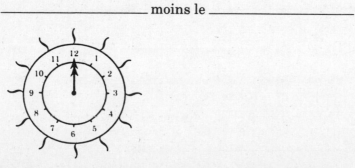

5. Il est _____

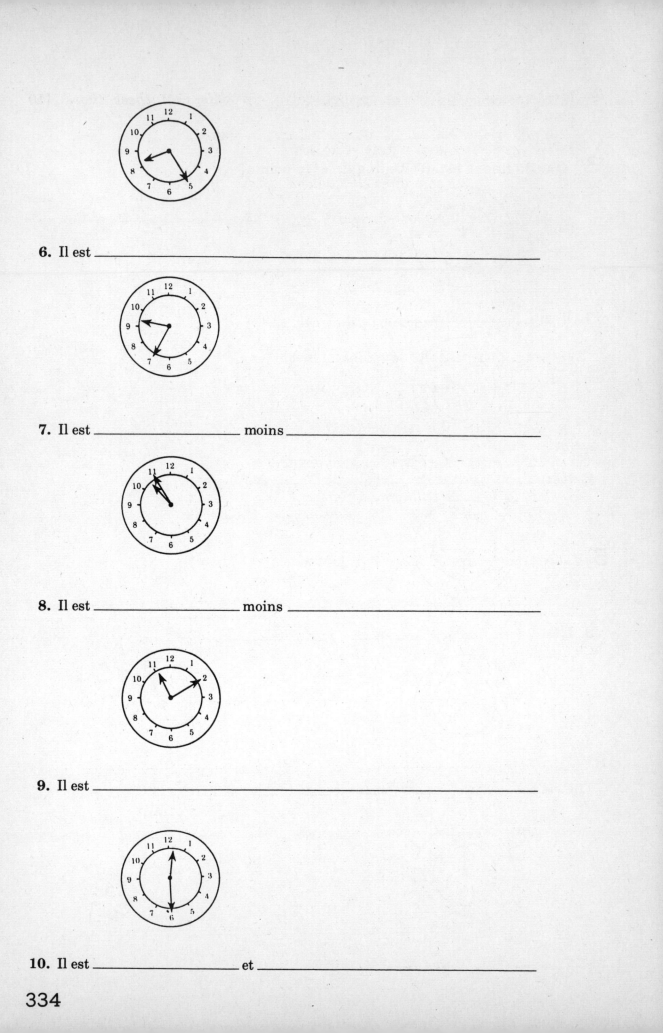

6. Il est _____

7. Il est _____ moins _____

8. Il est _____ moins _____

9. Il est _____

10. Il est _____ et _____

4 Demonstrative Adjectives: **ce, cet, cette, ces** (*this, that, these, those*). [10 points]

Fill in the correct demonstrative adjective:

1. _____ chambres sont jolies.

2. _____ eau est chaude.

3. _____ stade est magnifique.

4. _____ fromage est bon.

5. _____ carotte est délicieuse.

6. _____ salle de bains est bleue.

7. _____ pharmacie est bonne.

8. _____ blouses sont noires.

9. _____ sandwiches sont grands.

10. _____ éléphant est petit.

5 **Quel temps fait-il?** Expressions of weather [10 points]

1. _____   2. _____

3. _____   4. _____

5. _____ **6.** _____

7. _____ **8.** _____

9. _____ **10.** _____

6 Numbers [10 points]

Write the following numbers in French:

1. (11) _____ maisons

2. (13) _____ livres

3. (30) _____ élèves

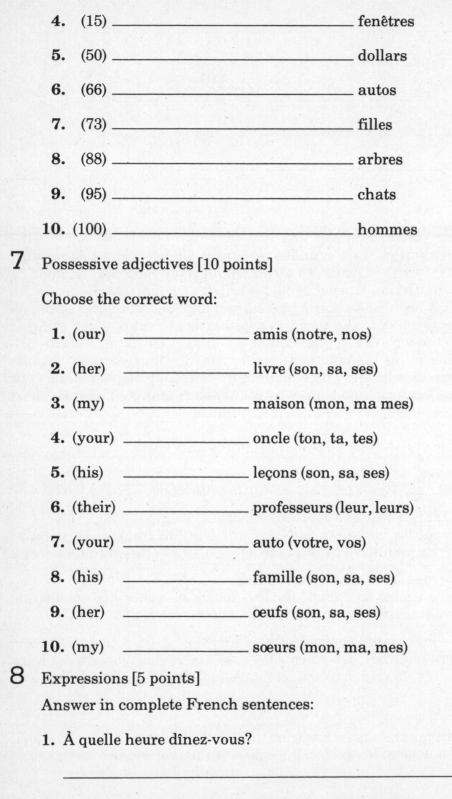

4. (15) _____ fenêtres

5. (50) _____ dollars

6. (66) _____ autos

7. (73) _____ filles

8. (88) _____ arbres

9. (95) _____ chats

10. (100) _____ hommes

7 Possessive adjectives [10 points]

Choose the correct word:

1. (our) _____ amis (notre, nos)

2. (her) _____ livre (son, sa, ses)

3. (my) _____ maison (mon, ma mes)

4. (your) _____ oncle (ton, ta, tes)

5. (his) _____ leçons (son, sa, ses)

6. (their) _____ professeurs (leur, leurs)

7. (your) _____ auto (votre, vos)

8. (his) _____ famille (son, sa, ses)

9. (her) _____ œufs (son, sa, ses)

10. (my) _____ sœurs (mon, ma, mes)

8 Expressions [5 points]

Answer in complete French sentences:

1. À quelle heure dînez-vous?

_____

2. Combien de personnes y a-t-il dans votre famille?

_____

3. Quel temps fait-il aujourd'hui?

_____

4. Quelle langue parlez-vous?

_____

5. De quelle couleur sont vos chaussures?

_____

9 Reading Comprehension [10 points]

C'est le premier juillet. Les grandes vacances commencent! Monsieur, Madame, Jean (15 ans) et Anne (13 ans) Leblanc sont contents. Ils vont en France aujourd'hui. Maman pense à tous les articles français qu'elle désire: les gants, les robes et les blouses. Papa pense à son ami Georges Gautier et à sa famille. Les Gautier habitent à Paris, la capitale de la France. Jean et Anne veulent parler et jouer avec Roger Gautier (16 ans) et Christine Gautier (12 ans). Les Gautier et les Leblanc vont visiter tous les musées et les grands monuments de cette belle ville. Ils vont prendre beaucoup de photos. Ils vont aussi dîner dans beaucoup de bons restaurants pour manger des spécialités françaises. Oh là là! Quelles vacances magnifiques!

Choose the correct answer by circling the appropriate letter:

1. Quelle saison est-ce?
(a) l'automne (b) l'été (c) l'hiver (d) le printemps

2. Pourquoi la famille Leblanc est-elle contente?
(a) Ils célèbrent les vacances de Noël. (b) Un ami français arrive à la maison. (c) La famille va faire un voyage. (d) Les classes commencent.

3. Qu'est-ce que maman désire faire à Paris?
(a) Elle désire visiter sa sœur. (b) Elle désire chercher des vêtements.
(c) Elle désire étudier le français. (d) Elle désire travailler.

4. Qu'est-ce que les enfants veulent faire à Paris?
(a) Ils veulent chercher des vêtements. (b) Ils veulent jouer avec leurs camarades. (c) Ils veulent écouter la musique populaire. (d) Ils veulent danser.

5. Qu'est-ce que les deux familles vont faire?
(a) Elles vont manger des repas français. (b) Elles vont jouer au tennis.
(c) Elles vont visiter les écoles. (d) Elles vont nager dans une grande piscine.

Vocabulaire français-anglais

A

à to, at; **à bientôt** see you soon; **à côté de** next to; **à tout à l'heure** see you later; **à votre service** at your service

accident m. accident

accord m. agreement; **d'accord** O.K., all right

acheter to buy

acteur m. actor

activité f. activity

actrice f. actress

addition f. bill, check

adjectif m. adjective

adorer to adore

aéroport m. airport

affreux (f. **affreuse**) terrible, awful

africain African

âge m. age

âgé old

agent de police m. policeman

aider to help

aïe! ouch!

aimable likable

aimer to like, to love

aliment m. food

Allemagne f. Germany

allemand German; m. German (language)

aller to go; **to be** (of health); **aller bien** to be well; **aller mal** to be ill

alors so

ambassadeur m. ambassador

américain American

ami m. friend

amour m. love

amuser to amuse; **s'amuser** to have a good time

an m. year

ananas m. pineapple

âne m. jackass, mule

anglais English; m. English (language)

Angleterre f. England

animal m. animal

animé animated

année f. year

anniversaire m. birthday

août m. August

appartement m. apartment

appeler to call; **s'appeler** to call oneself, to be called, to be named

applaudir to applaud

apporter to bring

apprendre to learn

après after

après-midi m. afternoon

arbre m. tree

argent m. money

arranger to arrange

arriver to arrive

artiste m. & f. artist

aspirine f. aspirin

assiette f. plate

associé m. associate

attendre to wait (for)

attention! (be) careful!

au, aux to the

aujourd'hui today

au revoir good-bye

aussi also

auteur m. author

autobus m. bus

automne m. autumn, fall

automobile f. car

autre other; **un/une autre** another

avant before

avec with

avocat m., **avocate** f. lawyer

avoir to have; **avoir ___ ans** to be ___ years old; **avoir besoin de** to need; **avoir chaud** to be warm, hot; **avoir faim** to be hungry; **avoir froid** to be cold; **avoir le hoquet** to have the hiccups; **avoir peur** to be afraid; **avoir raison** to be right; **avoir soif** to be thirsty; **avoir sommeil** to be sleepy; **avoir tort** to be wrong

avril m. April

B

banane f. banana

banque f. bank

beau (f. **belle**) handsome, beautiful; **faire beau** to be beautiful (weather)

beaucoup a lot, many; **beaucoup de** a lot of, many

bébé m. baby

beurre m. butter

bibliothèque f. library

bicyclette f. bicycle

bien well; **bien sûr** of course

bientôt soon; **à bientôt** see you soon
bifteck *m.* steak
blanc (*f.* **blanche**) white
bleu blue
blond blond
blouse *f.* blouse
boeuf *m.* beef
boire to drink
bon (*f.* **bonne**) good
bonne *f.* maid
bonjour hello
bonsoir good evening
bouche *f.* mouth
boucherie *f.* butcher shop
bouillabaisse *f.* fish soup
boulangerie *f.* bakery
bouteille *f.* bottle
boutique *f.* boutique, store
bras *m.* arm
brise *f.* breeze
bruit *m.* noise
brun brown; brunette
bureau *m.* bureau, desk

C

ça va? how's it going?; **ça va** everything's fine, O.K.
cacahouète *f.* peanut
café *m.* café, coffee
cahier *m.* notebook
campagne *f.* country
Canada *m.* Canada
canadien (*f.* **canadienne**) Canadian
carotte *f.* carrot
carte *f.* card, map; **carte postale** postcard
cathédrale *f.* cathedral
ce this, that
ceinture *f.* belt
cela that
célèbre famous
cent one hundred
centime *m.* cent
céréale *f.* cereal
cerise *f.* cherry
certain certain
certainement certainly
ces these, those
c'est this is, it is, he is, she is
ce sont these are, they are
central central
cet this, that
cette this, that
chaise *f.* chair
chambre *f.* room, bedroom
chance *f.* luck
chanson *f.* song
chanter to sing

chanteur *m.* singer
chapeau *m.* hat
chaque each
charmant charming
chat *m.* cat
château *m.* castle
chaud warm, hot; **avoir chaud** to be warm/hot; **faire chaud** to be warm/hot (weather)
chaussette *f.* sock
chaussure *f.* shoe
chef *m.* chef
chemise *f.* shirt
chercher to look for, to search
chéri *m.* darling
cheval *m.* horse
cheveux *m. pl.* hair
chèvre *f.* goat
chez at the house of
chien *m.* dog
Chine *f.* China
chinois Chinese; **le chinois** Chinese (language)
chocolat *m.* chocolate
choisir to choose
chose *f.* thing
cinéma *m.* movie theater
cinq five
cinquante fifty
cirque *m.* circus
citron *m.* lemon
classe *f.* class
client *m.* client
cochon *m.* pig
coeur *m.* heart
cognac *m.* cognac
combien how many, much; **combien de** how many, how much
combinaison *f.* combination
comme like, as; **comme ci comme ça** so, so
commencer (**à**) to begin (to)
comment how; **comment allez-vous?** how are you?; **comment vous appelez-vous?** what is your name?
compétition *f.* competition
complet *m.* (man's) suit
compter to count
confortable comfortable
content happy, content
conversation *f.* conversation
corps *m.* body
costume *m.* (woman's) suit, costume
cou *m.* neck
courant *m.* current
cours *m.* course
courir to run
court short
cousin *m.* cousin
couteau *m.* knife

couvert *m.* set table, table setting
craie *f.* chalk
cravate *f.* tie
crayon *m.* pencil
création *f.* creation
créature *f.* creature
créer to create
crème *f.* cream
créole creole
criminel *m.* criminal
cruel (*f.* cruelle) cruel
cuiller *f.* spoon
cuisine *f.* kitchen
cuisinier *m.* cook

D

d'abord at first
d'accord O.K., I agree
dans in
danse *f.* dance
danser to dance
de of, from; de rien you're welcome
décembre *m.* December
décider to decide
défendre to defend; se défendre to defend
   oneself
définition *f.* definition
déjà already
déjeuner *m.* lunch
délicieux (*f.* délicieuse) delicious
demain tomorrow
demander to ask
demeurer to live
demi half; une demi-heure a half hour
demoiselle *f.* young lady
dent *f.* tooth
dentiste *m. & f.* dentist
des some, of the
désastre *m.* disaster
descendre to go down, to get off
description *f.* description
désirer to want, to desire
dessert *m.* dessert
dessin *m.* design
détester to hate
deux two
devoirs *m. pl.* homework
dictionnaire *m.* dictionary
Dieu *m.* God
différent different
difficile difficult
dimanche *m.* Sunday
dîner *m.* dinner
dîner to dine, to have dinner
dire to say
discothèque *f.* discotheque
disque *m.* record

divan *m.* sofa
diviser to divide
dix ten
dix-huit eighteen
dix-neuf nineteen
dix-sept seventeen
docteur *m.* doctor
doigt *m.* finger
dollar *m.* dollar
domestique domesticated, trained
donner to give
douzaine *f.* dozen
douze twelve
droit right; à droite on the right, to the right
drôle funny
du some of the
dynamique dynamic

E

eau *f.* water
échapper to escape
école *f.* school
écouter to listen (to)
écrire to write
édifice *m.* building
église *f.* church
électricité *f.* electricity
élégant elegant
éléphant *m.* elephant
élève *m. & f.* student
elle she
elles they
employer to use, to employ
en in; en ville in the city, downtown; en
   retard late
encore yet, still, more; encore une
   fois again
endroit *m.* place
enfant *m. & f.* child
enfin finally
ennemi *m.* enemy
énorme enormous
entendre to hear
entrer to enter
envoyer to send
épice *f.* spice
épinards *m. pl.* spinach
escalier *m.* stairs
Espagne *f.* Spain
espagnol Spanish; *m.* Spanish (language)
essence *f.* gas
estomac *m.* stomach
et and
étage *m.* floor
États-Unis *m. pl.* United States
été *m.* summer
être to be

étude *f.* study
étudiant *m.*, étudiante *f.* student
étudier to study
examen *m.* test
excellent excellent
exceptionnel (*f.* exceptionnelle) exceptional
exciter to excite
exercice *m.* exercise
exportation *f.* exportation
expression *f.* expression
exquis exquisite
extraordinaire extraordinary

F

facile easy
facteur *m.* mailman
factrice *f.* mail carrier
faim *f.* hunger; avoir faim to be hungry
faire to make, do; faire beau to be beautiful weather; faire chaud to be hot (weather); faire froid to be cold (weather); faire le ménage to do (the) housework; faire une promenade to take a walk; faire du soleil to be sunny; faire du vent to be windy; faire un voyage to take a trip
famille *f.* family
faux (*f.* fausse) false
favori (*f.* favorite) favorite
femme *f.* woman, wife
fenêtre *f.* window
ferme *f.* farm
fermer to close
féroce ferocious
fête *f.* holiday, feast
feuilleton mélodramatique *m.* soap opera
février *m.* February
fièvre *f.* fever
figure *f.* face
fille *f.* girl, daughter
film *m.* film
fils *m.* son
finir to finish
fleur *f.* flower
fois times
formidable terrific
fort strong
fou (*f.* folle) crazy
fourchette *f.* fork
français French; *m.* French (language); Français *m.* Frenchman
France *f.* France
frère *m.* brother
froid cold; avoir froid to be cold; faire froid to be cold (weather)
fromage *m.* cheese
fruit *m.* fruit

G

gagner to earn; to win
gant *m.* glove
garçon *m.* boy; waiter
gare *f.* station
gâteau *m.* cake
gauche left; à gauche on the left, to the left
généralement generally
gens *m. pl.* people
gentil (*f.* gentille) nice
glace *f.* ice cream
gorille *m.* gorilla
goûter to taste
grâce à thanks to
grand big, large
grand-mère *f.* grandmother
grand-père *m.* grandfather
griller to grill; grillé grilled, toasted
grippe *f.* flu
gros (*f.* grosse) fat
groupe *m.* group
guide *m.* guide
guitare *f.* guitar

H

habiter to live in
Haïti *f.* Haiti
haïtien (*f.* haïtienne) Haitian
hamburger *m.* hamburger
haricot vert *m.* string bean
hélas alas
herbe *f.* grass
heure *f.* hour
hier yesterday
histoire *f.* history, story
hiver *m.* winter
homme *m.* man
hôpital *m.* hospital
hôtel *m.* hotel
huit eight

I

ici here
idée *f.* idea
identifier to identify
il he
île *f.* island
ils they
il y a there is, there are
immense immense, very big
immeuble *m.* apartment house
important important
impossible impossible
infirmier *m.* nurse

infirmière f. nurse
innocent innocent
intelligent intelligent
intéressant interesting
international international
invitation f. invitation
inviter to invite
Italie f. Italy
italien (f. **italienne**) Italian; m. Italian
   (language)
ivre drunk

J

jamais ever; **ne . . . jamais** never
jambe f. leg
jambon m. ham
janvier m. January
Japon m. Japan
japonais Japanese; m. Japanese (language)
jardin m. garden; **jardin zoologique** zoo
jaune yellow
je I
jeter to throw
jeudi m. Thursday
jeune young
joli pretty
jouer to play
jour m. day
jour d'Action de grâce m. Thanksgiving Day
journal m. newspaper
journée f. day
juillet m. July
juin m. June
jupe f. skirt
jus m. juice

L

l', la the
là there
laboratoire m. laboratory
laid ugly
laine f. wool
lait m. milk
laitue f. lettuce
lampe f. lamp
langue f. language, tongue
lapin m. rabbit
le the
leçon f. lesson
légume m. vegetable
lendemain m. next day
les the
lettre f. letter
leur, leurs their
lever to raise; **se lever** to arise, to get up
lèvre f. lip

lieu m. place, setting
lion m. lion
lire to read
liste f. list
lit m. bed
livre m. book
loin far; **loin de** far from
long (f. **longue**) long
loup m. wolf
lundi m. Monday
lycée m. secondary school, high school

M

ma my
madame f. Mrs., madam, lady
mademoiselle f. Miss, miss
magasin m. store
magazine m. magazine
magnifique magnificent
mai m. May
maillot de bain m. bathing suit
main f. hand
maintenant now
mais but
maïs m. corn
maison f. house
maître m. master, (male) teacher
malade sick
maman f. mom
manger to eat
manteau m. coat
marché m. market
marcher to walk, to work, to function
mardi m. Tuesday
mari m. husband
mars m. March
match m. match
mathématiques m. pl. math
matin m. morning
mauvais bad
mauve purple
me (to) me
médecin m. doctor
médecine f. medicine
médicament m. medicine, medication
meilleur best
membre m. member
même same
ménage m. housekeeping; **faire le ménage**
   to do the housework
menotte f. handcuff; **passer les**
   menottes to put on handcuffs
menu m. menu
merci thank you
mercredi m. Wednesday
mère f. mother
mes my

mettre to put, to put on; **mettre le couvert** to set the table
mexicain Mexican
midi *m.* noon; **Midi** *m.* South (of France)
mille *m.* thousand
million *m.* million
mince skinny, thin
minuit *m.* midnight
minute *f.* minute
mode *f.* style; **à la mode** stylish, in style
moi me
moins minus, less
mois *m.* month
moment *m.* moment
mon my
monde *m.* world
monsieur *m.* Mr., sir, gentleman
monstre *m.* monster
monstrueux (*f.* **monstrueuse**) monstrous
montre *f.* watch
monument *m.* monument
moteur *m.* motor
mousse *f.* mousse
mouton *m.* sheep
moyen *m.* means, way
muscle *m.* muscle
musée *m.* museum
musique *f.* music

N

nager to swim
nappe *f.* table cloth
narrateur *m.* narrator
nation *f.* nation
national national
Nations unies *f. pl.* United Nations
navet *m.* turnip
ne . . . jamais never
ne . . . ni . . . ni neither . . . nor
ne . . . pas not
ne . . . rien nothing
nécessaire necessary
n'est-ce pas? isn't that so?
neige *f.* snow
neuf nine
nez *m.* nose
n'importe it doesn't matter
Noël *m.* Christmas
noir black
nom *m.* name
non no
nos our
notre our
nous we; **nous deux** the two of us
nouveau (*f.* **nouvelle**) new
novembre *m.* November
numéro *m.* number
nuit *f.* night

O

obéir to obey
observer to observe
océan *m.* ocean
octobre *m.* October
œil (*pl.* **yeux**) *m.* eye
œuf *m.* egg; **œufs durs** hard-boiled eggs; **œufs frits** fried eggs
officiel (*f.* **officielle**) official
offrir to offer
oiseau *m.* bird
omelette *f.* omelet
on one, a person
oncle *m.* uncle
onze eleven
opinion *f.* opinion
orange *f.* orange
orangeade *f.* orangeade
ordinaire ordinary
organisation *f.* organization
oreille *f.* ear
ou or
où where
oui yes
ouvrir to open; **ouvert** opened

P

pain *m.* bread
paire *f.* pair
pantalon *f.* pants
papier *m.* paper
Pâques *m. pl.* Easter
par by; **par exemple** for example
parc *m.* park
parce que because
pardon excuse me
parent *m.* parent
parfait perfect
parler to speak
partie *f.* game, part
partout everywhere
passer to spend (*time*); **passer les menottes** to put on handcuffs
patron *m.* boss
pauvre poor
payer to pay (for)
pays *m.* country
pêche *f.* peach
pendant during
penser to think
père *m.* father
personnage *m.* character
personne *f.* person
petit small; **petit déjeuner** *m.* breakfast; **petits pois** *m. pl.* peas
peut-être perhaps
pharmacie *f.* pharmacy

photo *f.* photograph, picture
pièce *f.* room, play
pied *m.* foot
pique-nique *m.* picnic
piscine *f.* pool
plage *f.* beach
plat *m.* dish
pleuvoir to rain; **il pleut** it is raining
plus de more than
plusieurs several
poils *m. pl.* (body) hair
poisson *m.* fish
pomme *f.* apple
pomme de terre *f.* potato
pompier *m.* fire fighter
populaire popular
porc *m.* pork
porte *f.* door
porter to wear; to carry
possible possible
poule *f.* chicken, hen
poulet *m.* chicken
pour for, in order to
pourboire *m.* tip, gratuity
pourquoi why
pouvoir to be able to, can
pratiquer to practice
prendre to take
préparer to prepare
près near; **près de** near
président *m.* president
printemps *m.* spring
prix *m.* price, prize
produit laitier *m.* milk product
prof, professeur *m.* teacher
programme *m.* program
promenade *f.* walk; **faire une promenade**
  to take a walk
propriétaire *m.* proprietor, owner, boss
protéger to protect; **se protéger** to protect
  oneself
pull-over *m.* pullover, sweater
punir to punish

Q

quand when
quarante forty
quart *m.* quarter
quartier *m.* quarter, neighborhood
quatorze fourteen
quatre four
quatre-vingts eighty
quatre-vingt-dix ninety
que what; **qu'est-ce que** what; **qu'est-ce
  qu'il y a d'autre?** what else (is there)?
quel (*f.* **quelle**) what, what a, which
quelque chose something
question *f.* question

qui who
quiche *f.* quiche
quinze fifteen
quotidien (*f.* **quotidienne**) daily

R

radio *f.* radio
radis *m.* radish
raison *f.* reason; **avoir raison** to be right
rapidement rapidly, quickly
recherche *f.* research
refuser to refuse
regarder to look at, to watch
règle *f.* rule, ruler
remplir to fill
renard *m.* fox
rendez-vous *m.* meeting
rentrée *f.* return
réparer to fix
repas *m.* meal
répondre to answer
réponse *f.* answer
restaurant *m.* restaurant
reste *m.* remainder, rest
rester to stay
riche rich
rire to laugh
riz *m.* rice
robe *f.* dress
rouge red
rue *f.* street
russe Russian; *m.* Russian (language)
Russie *f.* Russia

S

sa his, her, its
sac *m.* bag, pocketbook
saison *f.* season
salade *f.* salad
sale dirty
salle *f.* room; **salle à manger** dining room;
  salle de bains bathroom
saluer to greet
salut hi!
samedi *m.* Saturday
sandwich *m.* sandwich
sans without
saucisson *m.* sausage
sauter to jump
sauvage savage
savant *m.* scientist
savoir to know (*a fact*)
scientifique scientific
secrétaire *m. & f.* secretary
seize sixteen
sel *m.* salt

selon according to
semaine *f.* week
sept seven
septembre *m.* September
sérieux (*f.* **sérieuse**) serious
serveuse *f.* waitress
service *m.* service; **à votre service** at your
  service
serviette *f.* napkin, towel
servir to serve
ses his, her, its
seul alone, only
seulement only
s'il te plaît, s'il vous plaît please
singe *m.* monkey
six six
sociable sociable
sœur *f.* sister
soif *f.* thirst; **avoir soif** to be thirsty
soir *m.* evening
soixante sixty
soixante-dix seventy
soleil *m.* sun; **faire du soleil** to be sunny
sommeil *m.* sleep; **avoir sommeil** to be
  sleepy
son his, her, its
sorte *f.* sort, type, kind
souffrir to suffer
soulier *m.* shoe
soupe *f.* soup
souris *f.* mouse
sous under
spécialité *f.* specialty
splendide splendid
sport *m.* sport
stade *m.* stadium
stupide stupid
stylo *m.* (ball-point) pen
sucre *m.* sugar
sud *m.* south
Suisse *f.* Switzerland
superbe superb
supermarché *m.* supermarket
sur on
sûr sure; **bien sûr** of course
surpris surprised
surprise-partie *f.* party, surprise party
surtout especially
sympathique nice

T

ta your
table *f.* table
tableau *m.* picture; chalk board
tante *f.* aunt
tard late
tasse *f.* cup

taxi *m.* taxi
téléphone *m.* telephone
télévision *f.* television
temps *m.* weather **Quel temps fait-il?** What
  is the weather?
terre *f.* earth, ground
terreur *f.* terror
terrible terrible
tes your
tête *f.* head
texte *m.* text, book
théâtre *m.* theater
thon *m.* tunafish
tigre *m.* tiger
timide timid, shy
titre *m.* title
toi *you*
tomate *f.* tomato
ton your
toujours always
tous all
Toussaint *f.* All Saint's Day
tout all, everything; **à tout à l'heure** see
  you later; **tout à coup** all of a sudden,
  suddenly; **tout de suite** immediately; **tout
  le monde** everybody; **tout le temps** all
  the time
tragique tragic
train *m.* train
transport *m.* transportation
travail *m.* work
travailler to work
treize thirteen
trente thirty
très very
triste sad
trois three
trop (de) too much, too many
tropical tropical
trouver to find
tu you
typique typical

U

un, une a, an
université *f.* university
usine *f.* factory
utiliser to use

V

vacances *f. pl.* vacation
vache *f.* cow
vanille *f.* vanilla
valoir to be worth; **il vaut** it is worth

vendeur *m.* vendor, seller
vendre to sell
vendredi *m.* Friday
venir to come
vent *m.* wind; **faire du vent** to be windy
verre *m.* glass
vert green
veston *m.* jacket
vêtements *m. pl.* clothes
viande *f.* meat
vie *f.* life
vieux (*f.* vieille) old
village *m.* village
ville *f.* city
vin *m.* wine
vingt twenty
visiter to visit
vite quickly
vivre to live
voici here is, here are

voilà there is, there are
voir to see
voleur *m.* thief
vos your
votre your
vouloir to wish, to want
vous you
voyage *m.* trip
vrai true

Y

yeux eyes

Z

zoo *m.* zoo

Vocabulaire anglais-français

A

a, an un, une
able: be able pouvoir
accident accident *m.*
according to selon
actor acteur *m.*
activity activité *f.*
actress actrice *f.*
adjective adjectif *m.*
adore adorer
afraid: be afraid avoir peur
African africain
after après
afternoon aprés-midi *m.*
again encore une fois
age âge *m.*
agreement accord *m.*; **agreed** d'accord
airplane avion *m.*
airport aéroport *m.*
alas hélas
all tout, toute, tous, toutes; **all the time** tout le temps; **All Saint's Day** La Toussaint
alone seul
already déjà
also aussi
always toujours
ambassador ambassadeur *m.*
American américain
amuse amuser; **to amuse oneself** s'amuser
and et
animal animal *m.*
animated animé(e)
another un/une autre
answer répondre; réponse *f.*
apartment appartement *m.*
apartment house immeuble *m.*
applaud applaudir
apple pomme *f.*
April avril *m.*
arm bras *m.*
arrange arranger
arrive arriver
artist artiste *m. & f.*
ask demander
aspirin aspirine *f.*
associate associé *m.*, associée *f.*
at a
August août *m.*

aunt tante *f.*
author auteur *m.*
autumn automne *m.*

B

baby bébé *m.*
bad mauvais
bag sac *m.*
bakery boulangerie *f.*
banana banane *f.*
bank banque *f.*
bathing suit maillot de bain *m.*
bathroom salle de bains *f.*
be être; **be able** pouvoir; **be careful** attention!; **be ill** aller mal; **be well** aller bien
beach plage *f.*
because parce que
bed lit *m.*
beef bœuf *m.*
before avant
begin (to) commencer (à)
belong to être à
belt ceinture *f.*
best meilleur
bicycle bicyclette *f.*
big grand
bird oiseau *m.*
birthday anniversaire *m.*
black noir
blond blond
blouse blouse *f.*
blue bleu
board tableau *m.*
body corps *m.*
book livre *m.*
boss patron *m.*, propriétaire *m. & f.*
bottle bouteille *f.*
bouillabaisse bouillabaisse *f.*
boutique boutique *f.*
boy garçon *m.*
bread pain *m.*
breakfast petit déjeuner *m.*
breeze brise *f.*
bring apporter
brother frère *f.*
brown, brunette brun

348

building édifice *m.*
bus autobus *m.*
but mais
butcher shop boucherie *f.*
butter beurre *m.*
buy acheter
by par

C

café café *m.*
cake gâteau *m.*
call appeler; **be called/named** s'appeler
can peut, peuvent, peux, pouvez, pouvons
Canada Canada *m.*
Canadian canadien (*f.* canadienne)
car automobile *f.*, voiture *f.*
card carte *f.*; **postcard** carte postale
carrot carotte *m.*
castle château *m.*
cat chat *m.*
cathedral cathédrale *f.*
cent centime *m.*
central central
cereal céréale *f.*
certain certain
certainly certainement
chair chaise *f.*
chalk craie *f.*
chalk board tableau *m.*
character personnage *m.*
charming charmant
check addition *f.*
cheese fromage *m.*
chef chef *m.*
cherry cerise *f.*
chicken poule *f.*, poulet *m.*
child enfant *m. & f.*
China Chine *f.*
Chinese chinois
chocolate chocolat *m.*
choose choisir
Christmas Noël *m.*
church église *f.*
circus cirque *m.*
city ville *f.*; **in the city** en ville
class classe *f.*
client client *m.*
close fermer
clothes vêtements *m. pl.*
coat manteau *m.*
coffee café *m.*
cognac cognac *m.*
cold froid; **be cold** avoir froid; **be cold (weather)** faire froid
combination combinaison *f.*
comfortable confortable
competition compétition *f.*

confused confus(e)
content content
conversation conversation *f.*
cook cuisinier *m.*, cuisinière *f.*
corn maïs *m.*
costume costume *m.*
count compter
country pays *m.*; campagne *f.*
course cours *m.*
cousin cousin *m.*, cousine *f.*
cow vache *f.*
crazy fou (*f.* folle)
cream crème *f.*
create créer
creation création *f.*
creature créature *f.*
creole créole
criminal criminel *m.*
cruel cruel (*f.* cruelle)
cup tasse *f.*
current courant *m.*

D

daily quotidien (*f.* quotidienne)
dance danser; danse *f.*
darling chéri *m.*, chérie *f.*
daughter fille *f.*
day jour *m.*; journée *f.*, **the next day** le lendemain
December décembre *m.*
decide décider
defend défendre; **defend oneself** se défendre
definition définition *f.*
delicious délicieux (*f.* délicieuse)
dentist dentiste *m. & f.*
description description *f.*
design dessin *m.*
desk bureau *m.*
dessert dessert *m.*
dictionary dictionnaire *m.*
different différent
difficult difficile
dine dîner
dining room salle à manger *f.*
dinner dîner *m.*
dirty sale
disaster désastre *m.*
discotheque discothèque *f.*
dish plat *m.*
divide diviser
doctor docteur *m.*; médecin *m.*
dog chien *m.*
dollar dollar *m.*
domestic domestique
door porte *f.*
down: go down descendre

dozen douzaine *f.*
dress robe *f.*
drink boire
drunk ivre
during pendant
dynamic dynamique

E

each chaque
ear oreille *f.*
earn gagner
earth terre *f.*
Easter Pâques *m. pl.*
easy facile
eat manger
egg œuf *m.*; **hard-boiled eggs** œufs durs;
  fried eggs œufs frits
eight huit
eighteen dix-huit
eighty quatre-vingts
electricity électricité *f.*
elegant élégant
elephant éléphant *m.*
eleven onze
England Angleterre *f.*
English anglais; anglais *m.*
enemy ennemi *m.*
enormous énorme
enter entrer
escape échapper
especially surtout
evening soir *m.*; **good evening** bonsoir
ever jamais
every tout, toute, tous, toutes;
  everybody tout le monde;
  everything tout; **everywhere** partout
example exemple *m.*; **for example** par
  exemple
excellent excellent
exceptional exceptionnel (*f.* exceptionnelle)
excite exciter
excuse me pardon
exercise exercice *m.*
exportation exportation *f.*
expression expression *f.*
extraordinary extraordinaire
eye œil *m.* (*pl.* yeux)

F

face figure *f.*
factory usine *f.*
false faux (*f.* fausse)
family famille *f.*
famous célèbre
far loin; **far from** loin de

farm ferme *f.*
fat gros (*f.* grosse)
father pére *m.*
favorite favori (*f.* favorite)
February février *m.*
ferocious féroce
fifteen quinze
fifty cinquante
fill remplir
film film *m.*
finally enfin
find trouver
finger doigt *m.*
finish finir
fireman pompier *m.*
first: at first d'abord
fish poisson *m.*
five cinq
floor étage *m.*
flower fleur *f.*
flu grippe *f.*
food aliments *m. pl.*
foot pied *m.*
for pour; **for example** par exemple
fork fourchette *f.*
forty quarante
four quatre
fourteen quatorze
fox renard *m.*
France France *f.*
French français; français *m.*
Friday vendredi *m.*
friend ami *m.*, amie *f.*
from de
fruit fruit *m.*
function marcher
funny drôle

G

game partie *f.*, match *m.*
garden jardin *m.*
gas essence *f.*
generally généralement
German allemand; allemand *m.*
Germany Allemagne *f.*
girl fille *f.*
give donner
glass verre *m.*
glove gant *m.*
go aller
goat chèvre *f.*
God Dieu *m.*
good bon (*f.* bonne)
good-bye au revoir
gorilla gorille *m.*
grandfather grand-père *m.*
grandmother grand-mère *f.*

grass herbe *f.*
great superbe
green vert
greet saluer
grilled grillé
group groupe *m.*
guide guide *m.*
guitar guitare *f.*

H

hair cheveux *m. pl.*; (*body*) poils *m. pl.*
Haiti Haïti *f.*
Haitian haïtien (*f.* haïtienne)
half demi; a half hour une demi-heure
ham jambon *m.*
hamburger hamburger *m.*
hand main *f.*
handcuff menotte *f.*; handcuff passer les
  menottes à
handsome beau (*f.* belle)
happy content
hat chapeau *m.*
hate détester
have avoir; have a good time s'amuser;
  have need of avoir besoin de
head tête *f.*
hear entendre
heart cœur *m.*
he il; he is c'est
hello bonjour
help aider
her son, sa, ses
here ici; here is, here are voici
hi salut
hiccups hoquet *m.;* to have hiccups avoir le
  hoquet
his son, sa, ses
history histoire *f.*
holiday fête *f.*
homework les devoirs *m. pl.*
horse cheval *m.*
hospital hôpital *m.*
hot chaud; to be hot avoir chaud; to be hot
  (weather) faire chaud
hotel hôtel *m.*
hour heure *f.*
house maison *f.*; at the house of chez
housework ménage *m.;* do the
  housework faire le ménage
how comment; how are you comment allez-
  vous; how's it going? ça va? how
  many combien de
hundred cent
hunger faim *f.*
hungry: be hungry avoir faim
husband mari *m.*

I

I je
ice cream glace *f.*
idea idée *f.*
identify identifier
immediately tout de suite
immense immense
important important
impossible impossible
in en, dans; in order to pour
innocent innocent
intelligent intelligent
interesting intéressant
international international
invitation invitation *f.*
invite inviter
island île *f.*
isn't that so? n'est-ce pas?
it il, elle, le, la; it is c'est
Italy Italie *f.*
Italian italien (*f.* italienne)
its son, sa ses

J

jackass âne *m.*
jacket veston *m.*
January janvier *m.*
Japan Japon *m.*
Japanese japonais; japonais *m.*
juice jus *m.*
July juillet *m.*
jump sauter
June juin *m.*

K

kitchen cuisine *f.*
knife couteau *m.*
know savoir

L

laboratory laboratoire *m.*
lady: young lady demoiselle *f.*
lamp lampe *f.*
language langue *f.*
late tard, en retard
laugh rire
lawyer avocat *m.*, avocate *f.*
learn apprendre
left gauche; on/to the left à gauche
leg jambe *f.*
lesson leçon *f.*
letter lettre *f.*

lettuce laitue *f.*
library bibliothèque *f.*
life vie *f.*
like comme; (*verb*) aimer
likable aimable
lion lion *m.*
lip lèvre *f.*
list liste *f.*
listen écouter
live vivre; (*reside in*) demeurer, habiter
long long (*f.* longue)
look at regarder
look for chercher
love aimer; amour *m.*
lucky: to be lucky avoir de la chance
lunch déjeuner *m.*

M

magazine magazine *m.*
magnificent magnifique
mail carrier facteur *m.*, factrice *f.*
make faire
man homme *m.*
many beaucoup
March mars *m.*
market marché *m.*
master maître *m.*
match match
mathematics mathématiques *m. pl.*
matter: it doesn't matter n'importe
May mai *m.*
me moi
meal repas *m.*
means moyen *m.*
meat viande *f.*
medicine médecine *f.*; médicament *m.*
meeting rendez-vous *m.*
member membre *m.*
menu menu *m.*
Mexican mexicain
midnight minuit *f.*
milk lait *m.*
million million *m.*
minus moins
minute minute
miss mademoiselle *f.*
mister monsieur *m.*
modern moderne
moment moment *m.*
Monday lundi *m.*
money argent *m.*
monkey singe *m.*
monster monstre *m.*
monstrous monstrueux (*f.* monstrueuse)
month mois *m.*
monument monument *m.*
more plus; more than plus de

morning matin *m.*
mother mère *f.*, maman *f.*
motor moteur *m.*
mouse souris *f.*
mousse mousse *f.*
mouth bouche *f.*
movies cinéma *m.*
Mrs. madame, Mme
muscle muscle *m.*
museum musée *m.*
music musique *f.*
my mon, ma, mes

N

name nom *m.*; what is your
    name? comment vous appelez-vous? my
    name is je m'appelle
napkin serviette *f.*
nation nation *f.*
national national
near près; near to près de
necessary nécessaire
neck cou *m.*
need avoir besoin de
neither . . . nor ne . . . ni . . . ni
never ne . . . jamais
new nouveau (*f.* nouvelle)
newspaper journal *m.*
nice sympathique, gentil (*f.* gentille),
    aimable
night nuit *f.*
nine neuf
nineteen dix-neuf
ninety quatre-vingt-dix
no non
noise bruit *m.*
noon midi *m.*
nose nez *m.*
not ne . . . pas
notebook cahier *m.*
nothing ne . . . rien
November novembre *m.*
now maintenant
nurse infirmière *f.*
number numéro

O

observe observer
obey obéir
ocean océan *m.*
October octobre *m.*
of de; of course bien sûr
offer offrir
official officiel (*f.* officielle)
O.K. d'accord, ça va

old âgé, vieux (*f.* vieille)
omelet omelette *f.*
on sur
one (a person) on
only seulement, seul
open ouvrir; **opened** ouvert
opinion opinion *f.*
or ou
orange orange *f.*
orangeade orangeade *f.*
order: in order to pour
ordinary ordinaire
organization organisation *f.*
other autre
our notre, nos
owner propriétaire *m.*

P

pair paire *f.*
pants pantalon *m.*
paper papier *m.*
parent parent *m.*
park parc *m.*
part partie *f.*
pay payer
peas petits pois *m. pl.*
peanut cacahouète *f.*
pen stylo *m.*
pencil crayon *m.*
people gens *m. pl.*
perfect parfait
perhaps peut-être
person personne *f.*
pharmacy pharmacie *f.*
photograph photographie *f.*
picnic pique-nique *m.*
picture tableau *m.*, photo *f.*
pig cochon *m.*
place lieu *m., endroit m.*
plate assiette *f.*
play jouer
please s'il te plaît, s'il vous plaît
pocketbook sac *m.*
policeman agent de police *m.*
pool piscine *m.*
poor pauvre
popular populaire
pork porc *m.*
possible possible
postcard carte postale *f.*
potato pomme de terre *f*
practice pratiquer
prepare préparer
president président *m.*
pretty joli
price, prize prix *m.*
program programme *m.*

protect protéger; **protect oneself** se protéger
pullover pull-over *m.*
punish punir
purple mauve
put mettre; **put on** mettre

Q

quarter quart *m.*
question question *f.*
quiche quiche *f.*
quickly vite, rapidement

R

rabbit lapin *m.*
radio radio *f.*
radish radis *m.*
rain pluie *f.*; **it's raining** il pleut
raise lever
rapidly rapidement, vite
read lire
reason raison *f.*
record disque *m.*
red rouge
remainder reste *m.*
repair réparer
research recherche *f.*
rest reste *m.*
restaurant restaurant *m.*
return rentrée *f.*
rice riz *f.*
rich riche
right droit *f.*; **onto the right** à droite
right: be right avoir raison
room chambre *f.*, salle *f.*, pièce *f.*
rule règle *f.*
ruler règle *f.*
run courir
Russia Russie *f.*
Russian russe; russe *m.*

S

sad triste
salad salade *f.*
salt sel *m.*
same même
sandwich sandwich *m.*
Saturday samedi *m.*
savage sauvage
say dire
school école *f.*; **high school** lycée *m.*
scientific scientifique
scientist savant *m.*, savante *f.*

season saison *f.*
secretary secrétaire *m. & f.*
see voir; **see you later** à toute à l'heure
sell vendre
send envoyer
September septembre *m.*
serious sérieux (*f.* sérieuse)
servant bonne *f.*
serve servir
service service *m.;* **at your service** à votre
  service
set the table mettre le couvert
setting lieu *m.*
seven sept
seventeen dix-sept
seventy soixante-dix
several plusieurs
she elle; **she is** c'est
sheep mouton *m.*
shirt chemise *f.*
shoe chaussure *f.;* soulier *m.*
short court
shy timide
sick malade
sing chanter
singer chanteur *m.*
sir monsieur
sister sœur *f.*
six six
sixteen seize
sixty soixante
skinny mince
skirt jupe *f.*
sleep sommeil *m.;* **to be sleepy** avoir
  sommeil
small petit
snow neige *f.;* **it's snowing** il neige
so alors; **so so** comme ci comme ça
soap opera feuilleton mélodramatique *m.*
sociable sociable
sock chaussette *f.*
sofa divan *m.*
something quelque chose
son fils *m.*
song chanson *f.*
soon bientôt; **see you soon** à bientôt
soup soupe *f.*
south sud *m.*
Spain Espagne *f.*
Spanish espagnol; espagnol *m.*
speak parler
speciality spécialité *f.*
spend (*time*) passer
spice épice *f.*
spinach épinards *m. pl.*
splendid splendide
spoon cuiller *f.*
sport sport *m.*
spring printemps *m.*

stadium stade *m.*
stairs escalier *m.*
station gare *f.*
stay rester
steak bifteck *m.*
still encore
stomach estomac *m.*
store magasin *m.,* boutique *f.*
story histoire *f.*
street rue *f.*
string bean haricot vert *m.*
strong fort
student élève *m. & f.;* étudiant *m.,* étudiante *f.*
study étudier; étude *f.*
stupid stupide
style mode *f.;* **stylish** à la mode
suddenly tout à coup
suffer souffrir
sugar sucre *m.*
suit complet *m.*
summer été *m.*
sun soleil *m.;* **to be sunny** faire du soleil
Sunday dimanche *m.*
supermarket supermarché *m.*
sure sûr
surprise surprise *f.;* **surprise**
  party surprise-partie *f.*
surprised surpris
swim nager
Switzerland Suisse *f.*

T

table table *f.;* **set the table** mettre le couvert
table cloth nappe *f.*
take prendre
taste goûter
taxi taxi *m.*
teacher professeur *m.,* maître *m.*
telephone téléphone *m.*
television télévision *f.*
ten dix
terrible terrible, affreux (*f.* affreuse)
terrific formidable
terror terreur *m.*
test examen *m.*
text texte *m.*
thanks to grâce à
thank you merci
that cela, ce, cet, cette
the le, la, les
theater théâtre *m.*
their leur, leurs
there là; **there is, there are** voilà, il y a
these ces
they ils, elles
thief voleur *m.*
thing chose *f.*

think penser
thirst soif *f.*; **to be thirsty** avoir soif
thirteen treize
thirty trente
this ce, cet, cette; **this is** c'est; **these are** ce sont
thousand mille
three trois
throw jeter
Thursday jeudi *m.*
tie cravate *f.*
tiger tigre *m.*
time temps *m.*; **have a good time** s'amuser
times fois
timid timide
tip pourboire *m.*
title titre *m.*
toasted grillé
to à, à l', à la, au, aux
today aujourd'hui
tomato tomate *f.*
tomorrow demain
too aussi; trop; **too much** trop de
tooth dent *f.*
train train *m.*
transportation transport *m.*
tree arbre *m.*
trip voyage; **take a trip** faire un voyage
tropical tropical
true vrai
Tuesday mardi *m.*
tunafish thon *m.*
turnip navet *m.*
twelve douze
twenty vingt
two deux; **the two of us** nous deux
type sorte *f.*
typical typique

U

ugly laid
uncle oncle *m.*
under sous
United Nations Nations unies *f. pl.*
United States États-Unis *m. pl.*
university université *f.*
use employer, utiliser

V

vacation vacances *f. pl.*
vanilla vanille *f.*
vegetable légume *m.*
vendor vendeur *m.*
very très
village village *m.*
visit visiter

W

wait (for) attendre
waiter garçon *m.*
waitress serveuse *f.*
walk marcher; promenade *f.*; **take a walk** faire une promenade
want désirer, vouloir
warm chaud; **to be warm** avoir chaud; **to be warm (weather)** faire chaud
watch regarder; montre *f.*
water eau *f.*
we nous
wear porter
weather temps *m.*; **what is the weather?** quel temps fait-il?
Wednesday mercredi *m.*
week semaine *f.*
welcome: you are welcome de rien
well bien
what que
what a quel, quelle
when quand
where où
white blanc (*f.* blanche)
who qui
why pourquoi
wife femme *f.*
win gagner
wind vent *m.*; **be windy** faire du vent
window fenêtre *f.*
wine vin *m.*
winter hiver *m.*
wish vouloir, désirer
with avec
without sans
wolf loup *m.*
woman femme *f.*
wool laine *f.*
work travailler, marcher; travail *m.*
world monde *m.*
worth: it is worth il vaut
write écrire

Y

year an *m.*, année *f.*
yellow jaune
yes oui
yesterday hier
yet encore
you tu, vous, toi
young jeune
your votre, vos, ton, ta, tes

Z

zoo zoo *m.*, jardin zoologique *m.*

Index

adjectives
  agreement 296–297, 325
  demonstrative 220–221, 225
  descriptive 43–50, 58; position 52–53, 296–297, 325
  of color 295–297
  of nationality 314, 320–322
  possessive 206–209, 211–212, 224–225
aller 252–253, 271
  expressions with 252–253, 271
  followed by infinitive 253
animals 302–303
arithmetic 94
article, *see* definite article, indefinite article
au (contraction of **à** + **le**) 246, 270
aux (contraction of **à** + **les**) 246, 270
avoir 140, 159
  expressions with 143, 160

be, expressed in French 120

calendar 149
clothes 292–293
colors 295–297
conjugation 68–69, 103
contractions 245–247, 270
countries 314
  expressing *to* and *from* with 315–316

dates 155–156
days of the week 149, 160
de, partitive use 181–183
definite article
  plural 23–24, 58
  singular 10, 58
demonstrative adjectives 220–221, 225
des (contraction of **de** + **les**) 246, 270
  partitive meaning 181–182
du (contraction of **de** + **le**) 246–270
  partitive meaning 181–182

-er verbs 65, 68–70, 77
être 120, 159

faire 262–263, 271
  with weather expressions 261–263, 271
foods 175–176

gender (feminine and masculine) 10

indefinite article 36–37, 58
  omission 118
interrogative sentences 80, 82–84, 103–104
-ir verbs 97–99, 104

l', la, le 7–10, 58
languages 314
les 23–24, 58

months 149, 151–152

negation 78–79, 103, 160
  with partitive 183
nouns
  feminine and masculine 7–10, 36–37
  plural of 23–24, 37, 58
numbers 90, 104, 233, 270

partitive 181, 183, 224
parts of the body 133
plural of nouns 23–24, 37, 58
possessive adjectives 206–209, 211–212, 224–225
pouvoir 285, 325
pronouns, subject 66–67, 103
pronunciation 1–3

questions 80, 82–84, 103–104

-re verbs 125–127, 159

seasons 153, 160
subject pronouns 66–67

the, expressed in French 7–10, 23–24
time expressions 189–193, 197, 199, 224
tu, compared with **vous** 66

un, une 36–37, 58

verbs
   aller 252–253, 271; expressions with 252–253, 271; followed by infinitive 253

avoir 140, 159; expressions with 143, 160
-er verbs 65, 68–70, 77, 103
être 119–120, 159
faire 262–263, 271; with weather expressions 261–263, 271
-ir verbs 97–99, 104
pouvoir 285
-re verbs 125–127, 159
voir 309, 325
vouloir 285, 325
vous, compared with **tu** 66

weather expressions 261–263